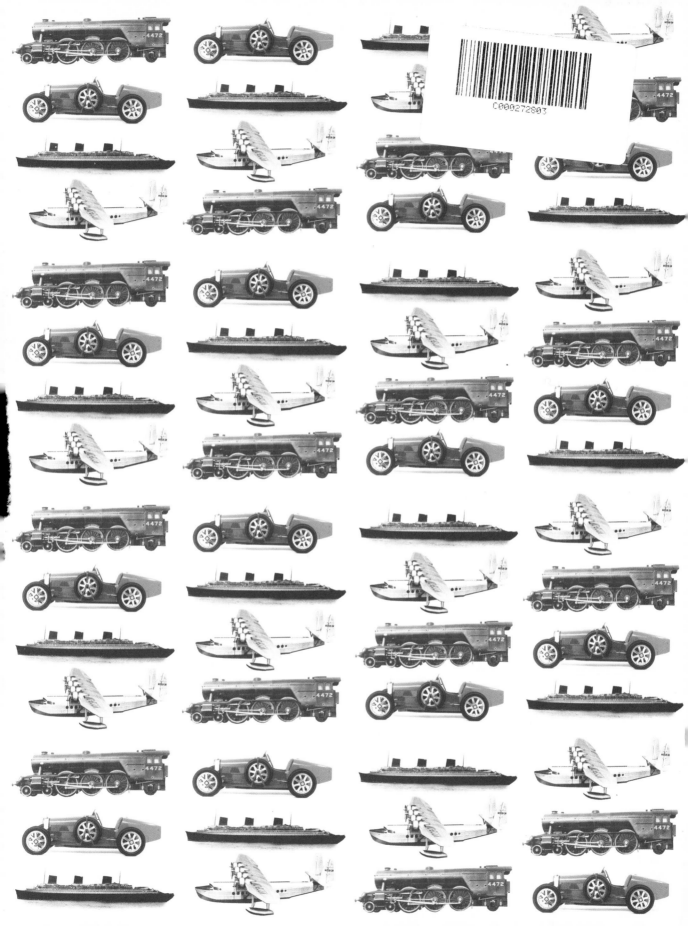

TRAINS, PLANES, SHIPS & CARS

ALSO BY JAMES HAMILTON-PATERSON

NON-FICTION

Playing with Water

Three Miles Down

Seven-Tenths: The Sea and its Thresholds

America's Boy

Empire of the Clouds: When Britain's Aircraft Ruled the World

Marked for Death: The First War in the Air

Eroica: The First Great Romantic Symphony

Blackbird: The Untouchable Spy Plane

What We Have Lost: The Dismantling of Great Britain

FICTION

The View from Mount Dog

Gerontius

The Bell Boy

Griefwork

Ghosts of Manila

The Music

Loving Monsters

Cooking with Fernet Branca

Amazing Disgrace

Rancid Pansies

Under the Radar

TRAINS, PLANES, SHIPS & CARS

The Golden Age
1900 – 1941

James Hamilton-Paterson

HEAD of ZEUS

An Apollo Book

A catalogue record for this book is available from the British Library.

ISBN (HB): 9781789542363
ISBN (E): 9781789542356

Interior design by Akihiro Nakayama

Printed and bound in Spain by Graficas Estella

Head of Zeus Ltd
First Floor East
5–8 Hardwick Street
London EC1R 4RG
WWW.HEADOFZEUS.COM

Contents

INTRODUCTION
Speed, Style and Streamlining

Speed and elegance must have been associated in the human mind from the very beginning, surely for tens of millennia. Certainly cave painters appear to have revered and even fetishized the swift and powerful animals they hunted. Tens of thousands of years later we still admire a racehorse or greyhound at full stretch, a cheetah closing on its prey, the folded raptor as it stoops with a shriek of air. It is an atavistic pleasure that can bring with it a momentary, almost superstitious, chill.

In her book *The Living Mountain,* the late Scottish writer and hill-walker Nan Shepherd muses startlingly on the swiftness of the eagle and the peregrine falcon, the red deer and the hare, wondering why grace has been added to the severely practical necessity of speed. Perhaps 'the swoop, the parabola, the arrow-flight of hooves and wings' become lovely through their obedience to function so that 'Beauty is not adventitious but essential.'[1] In 1934 and in a wildly different context, the copywriters of Madison Avenue made the same point about Chrysler's new streamlined car. 'Old mother nature has always designed her creatures for the function they are to perform. You have only to look at a dolphin, a gull, or a greyhound to appreciate the rightness of the tapering, flowing contour of the new Airflow.'[2] Lyrical copy, even if the car failed to sell.

Nan Shepherd probably need not have wondered why 'grace' accompanies speed. We must be genetically engineered to view litheness as admirable, implying a pared-down, unencumbered quality. Even though the word 'streamline' dates from around 1870, the earliest hunter-gatherers would have observed how hawks gain speed by streamlining themselves when diving, wings folded and beak foremost. (The peregrine falcon has claims to be the fastest animal on earth, having been timed in a dive at 217 mph [349 kph].) Supposedly 'primitive' fisher-folk would have noticed that predator fish (sharks, tuna, mackerel, etc.) are shaped for speed rather than for cunning methods of camouflage in order to catch their prey. They might not have been able to measure a swordfish's top speed as 80 mph (129 kph) but they would have noticed a correlation between shape and velocity. It seems beyond argument that a respect and admiration for speed in nature should be hard-wired into the human psyche. As a burst of speed demands energy, it always contains an element of competitiveness – the quicker you are, the less likely you and your family are to go hungry. This basic truth undoubtedly lies behind our continued fascination with any form of speed, such that we have always stylised our instinct for predation by means of races. Being a kind of proxy hunt in which the winner might take over as the new tribal leader, racing each other soon extended beyond mere running to take in skill on horseback or in sailboats. In case anyone thinks there is something modern about a yacht or speedboat owner boasting of their craft's speed or elegance, they should remember the Roman poet Catullus:

> *My bean-pod boat you see here*
> > *friends & guests*
> *will tell you*
> > *if you ask her*
> *that she's been*
> > *the fastest piece of timber*
> *under oar or sail*
> > *afloat.[3]*

That elegance and speed often go hand in hand is an underlying assumption in this book, although the pairing will be moderated by what is technologically feasible at any given moment. Catullus's 'bean-pod' boat is a good description of a design that even then must have been ancient. A craft that is long, pointed at both ends and with a rounded bottom is clearly better designed for speed than a raft or barge. This shape, classically that of a canoe, must originally have been the result of much trial and error, backed up by biomimesis: the copying of shapes from archetypes in nature – in this case swift predators like swordfish or porpoises. When the early British pioneer of flight, George Cayley, proposed an airship in 1804 he gave its envelope the profile of a trout, reasoning that the trout had the best-shaped body for slipping through the air. The legend of the young Icarus is equally about biomimesis, since his father Daedalus stuck feathers to their bodies with wax for their attempted escape from Crete by flying. Similarly, in one of his sketches for a glider, Leonardo da Vinci gave it bat's wings. More recent examples of people hoping to fly also began with wings modelled on those of birds. This mimicry was quite conscious in Otto Lilienthal's successful designs for early hang gliders in the 1890s. It appeared equally so in the early Austrian powered aircraft, the Etrich-Rumpler Taube ('dove') which became Germany's first mass-produced military aircraft just before the First World War. Despite its remarkably birdlike appearance, it turns out that its wings were actually modelled on the seeds of a Javan cucumber that can cover considerable distances when dispersed on the wind. Even though the Taube's wings were not inspired by birds, they were undoubtedly biomimetic. Despite being an early flying machine with a rattly engine, its lines had a certain primordial elegance.

The Etrich-Rumpler Taube ('dove') became the world's first warplane in 1911, when an Italian pilot in Libya dropped hand grenades from it. By the First World War the type was already obsolete. This one, with an enclosed cockpit, was Rumpler's 'Dolphin' model.

◇◇◇◇◇◇◇◇◇◇◇◇◇◇◇◇◇◇◇◇◇◇◇◇◇◇

Yet merely imitating nature is not enough. As industrialisation rapidly increased in the nineteenth century, engineers needed to know in detail how water, steam or air flows in pipes and around obstructions. The basic physics had been established by Newton, but in 1738 Daniel Bernoulli published *Idrodinamica*, or 'Hydrodynamics', in which he expounded what soon became known as Bernoulli's Principle. This explained at length the behaviour of fluids – air as well as water – and was to become the basis of both aerodynamics and hydrodynamics. So important has his principle proved that, in 2002, Bernoulli was posthumously inducted into the San

Diego Air & Space Museum's Hall of Fame. It is this principle that explains why, when air moves faster over the curved upper surface of an aircraft's wing than it does over the flat underside, the pressure above the wing is less than that below and thus generates lift. In countless bathrooms the inward 'suck' of shower curtains towards the fast-flowing stream of water is an even more familiar daily testament to Bernoulli's insight.

In the latter half of the nineteenth century, naval architects increasingly needed to know exactly what happens when a stream of water flows around a ship's hull. By 1880 'streamlining' (although the word itself had barely been coined) became a matter for serious study, where speed was essential and competitive for clippers or battleships, racing yachts, sculls and liners. If at a practical level this mostly concerned shipwrights it was simply because no land vehicles such as trains or the earliest cars were yet fast enough to make questions of aerodynamics relevant, and powered flying machines (as opposed to Lilienthal's gliders) were still theoretical. Even so, George Cayley had built himself a machine with a whirling arm to measure the lift and drag of differently shaped wings. Its inherent drawback was that a simple revolving arm meant the model wing was always flying into the wake of its own turbulence. In 1871 two Britons, Frank Wenham and John Browning, built what was probably the world's first proper wind tunnel using a steam-powered blower. An article written by Wenham was spotted by the Smithsonian Institution, who recommended it to the Wright brothers. It almost certainly influenced the design of the 'Flyer', for in 1901 the Wrights also built themselves a small but effective wind tunnel to conduct their own tests of wing and propeller shapes. It was already clear that the more speed an aircraft had, the more lift its wings could generate.

By 1900 transatlantic passenger ships had become big business and were already highly competitive. The lucrative trade taking the flood of European emigrants over the ocean to America was such that owners needed their liners to make the crossing in the shortest possible turnaround time. Speed was thus essential, and in turn the design of the hull and propellers became critical – although new ideas often turned out to be difficult to implement because shipbuilding was an ancient craft and yards tended instinctively to adhere to traditional styles and working methods. This was especially true in Britain since, thanks to its immense empire as well as to having pioneered the Industrial Revolution, it had the world's biggest shipbuilding industry and merchant fleet. Any incentive for its shipyards to innovate was often frustrated by complacency and convention.

In both ships and locomotives everywhere steam still provided the motive force, but by 1900 the technology of steam power had largely peaked. Once it had developed enough for it to be clear that the internal combustion engine had superior power-to-weight ratio, smaller size and greater flexibility, it was merely a question of time before ships would also be driven by reciprocating engines. The one exception to this trend was that, following Charles Parsons' demonstration of his fast launch *Turbinia* in 1897, the steam turbine was developed as a smoother alternative to reciprocating engines, although before long its steam would be raised by oil-burning rather than by coal. The turbine itself gradually went in a separate direction, most notably as the principle of the jet engine.

Meanwhile on land the internal combustion engine was refined into a novel source of power. If we date the first automobile with an internal combustion engine to the Benz Patent-Motorwagen of 1885, it is extraordinary how rapidly the efficiency of this type of engine grew. It not only made the Wrights' powered flight possible in 1903 but promised increasingly fast and reliable terrestrial transport. Industrial technology was already associated with speed thanks to the invention of the steam locomotive in the early nineteenth

In 1885 Karl Benz's Patent-Motorwagen became the world's first car to be driven by a petrol engine.

century. In the first two decades of the twentieth century, however, speed itself became a commercial, social and even aesthetic marker, especially when associated with the new technologies of aircraft and cars.

Speed for speed's sake soon became its own message. As early as 1905, in their seminal work *Modern Advertising*, the Americans Earnest Elmo Calkins and Ralph Holden looked at the limited but ever-growing market for automobiles and saw the challenge of selling them as that of 'expressing the inexpressible, of suggesting not so much a motor car as *speed*'. The promise of fast and ubiquitous travel heralded a new technological, military, economic, political and social dawn: a revolution that was first eagerly embraced by pre-1914 artistic movements such as Futurism in Italy. In one way or another, speed would turn out to be the hallmark of the entire twentieth century.

◇◇◇◇◇◇◇◇◇◇◇◇◇◇◇◇◇◇◇◇◇◇◇◇◇

The builders of early aircraft soon realised that flying faster was not merely a matter of increased power but depended crucially on aerodynamics. Fast-moving air did indeed provide lift, but it also caused drag. The science of streamlining thus became increasingly important. The earliest automobile designers, on the other hand, had been dealing with such low speeds they hardly needed to take wind resistance into account. Their designs essentially took over that of horse-drawn vehicles, the limousine driver (like any coachman) being exposed to the elements for much of the first quarter of the twentieth century. Yet speed still implied competition and it was not long before people began racing each other in cars, the first official automobile race being held in Paris in 1894. Even so, in the case of cars the idea of streamlining was still more a developing aesthetic than an aerodynamic necessity. Henry Ford's land speed record of 1904 was achieved in his '999' car: a huge engine mounted on a bare wooden chassis with four wheels, no body and a crude brake. Ford steered while his mechanic operated the throttle. Together they set a new record of 91.37 mph (147.05 kph). The chief idea behind this vehicle's design was clearly to save weight rather than to minimise drag. A few judicious light fairings might have reduced wind resistance and enabled it to go still faster, although any gain would have been marginal.

Yet the concept of a highly streamlined vehicle had already flown in 1900, in the shape of Count Zeppelin's first dirigible airship, the LZ1. A massive structure 128 metres (420 ft) long with a diameter of only 11.75 metres (38.5 ft), it was a slender tube and thus shaped like a cigar – or better,

Henry Ford (standing)
and a mechabic (seated)
with Ford's '999' car in
which he set a new speed
record of 91.37 mph
(147.05 kph) on a frozen
lake in January 1904
– a feat that proved an
excellent advertisement
for his new company.

a cheroot. George Cayley would surely have recognised this as a plausible design for minimising air resistance even if it wasn't exactly trout-shaped. Successive airships confirmed that streamlining was an essential principle not only of flight but of anything built for speed. Even bullets had become pointed cylinders rather than balls. Once the idea of motor races and land speed records had taken hold it was clear that the designers of cars, aircraft and ships needed a sound understanding of the underlying physics. Speed meant science, science meant speed, and together they spelt the future.

As it happens, the first road vehicle to exceed 62 mph (100 kph) was not driven by an internal combustion engine but by electricity. In 1899 a torpedo-shaped Belgian electric vehicle with its driver sitting high up – and ruining its otherwise excellent aerodynamics – set a new world speed record of 65.8 mph (105.9 kph): much faster than any contemporary petrol-driven car. (It was still far slower than the best steam railway engine. That same year a German engine managed an amazing 130 mph [209 kph].) The Belgian electric vehicle was appealingly named *La Jamais Contente* ('The Never Satisfied'), and the bullet shape of its light alloy body was a clear indication that matters of wind resistance had been fully considered – even though the point had not yet been reached when the driver was included in the calculations.

Count Zeppelin's first airship, the LZ1, being towed out for its first flight on Bodensee in July 1900. The engines in the two gondolas drove four propellers via inefficiently long drive shafts.

In the image on the vehicle: "DE CAMILLE JENATZY / RECORD DU MONDE 1899 PAR 105 KM A L'HEURE / AVEC ACCUMULATEURS FULMEN / 1899"

This vehicle is also a reminder that, at the turn of the twentieth century, not only were half of all cars electric and not petrol-driven, but in New York alone there were already 16,000 charging stations. Apart from being quieter, mechanically simpler, faster and much easier to drive, electric cars had the further enormous advantage of reliability. Petrol-driven cars of the day constantly broke down, and if they didn't, they usually had to stop every 20 miles or so to allow the engine to cool. Electric runabouts such as the Baker Electric of 1910 were such that a New York lady might use one for her shopping, steering it herself by means of a tiller. It was claimed to have a range of 100 miles (161 km) between charging. The reason petrol overtook electricity for motive power was simply because it became a lot cheaper. In every other respect – especially in terms of pollution – electricity was much superior. It is wholly ironic that, 120 years later and in one form or another, it is being seen as the future of all terrestrial transport.

In 1899 the charmingly named Belgian electric car, *La Jamais Contente*, became the first road vehicle ever to exceed 62 mph (100 kph): a new land speed record.

The importance of streamlining and aerodynamics was thus appreciated well before the First World War and physicists considered the ideal design for the least wind resistance to be teardrop-shaped, with the bulbous side foremost. This can be seen in an extraordinary futuristic car produced in Italy in 1913, the prototype Alfa Castagna Aerodinamica. It was beautifully finished in swirl-pattern polished aluminium, leaving only the four wheels exposed and unshrouded. With its curved, flush (but not yet shatterproof) windscreen, porthole windows and pointed tail it was twenty years ahead of its time, as can be seen by comparing it with the model of a streamlined car made by the American designer Norman Bel Geddes in 1932. As it offered the least wind resistance, the teardrop or bubble shape for vehicles of all kinds became one of the essential components of the 'streamline moderne' style. Although this was to dominate American industrial design in the 1930s with examples like Buckminster Fuller's Dymaxion Car No. 3, it had several precursors apart from the Italian Aerodinamica car. Even the cover of *Scientific American*'s 5 January 1918 issue showed a futuristic bubble-style car billed as the 'Motorist's Dream'.

Opposite: A Baker Electric runabout of 1910. With its silence, mechanical simplicity and lack of exhaust fumes it was unquestionably a graceful way of getting around.

The Alfa Castagna Aerodinamica of 1913 – years ahead of its time in terms of overall streamlining.

Top: Norman Bel Geddes' Motorcar No. 9 of 1933. He was already famous for his streamlined industrial designs and this model's number was his estimation of how many years ahead of its time it was.

Bottom: Buckminster Fuller's concept car, the Dymaxion No. 3, on display in 1934 at the World's Fair in Chicago. Its Ford V-8 engine allied to the aerodynamic 'teardrop' shape reportedly gave it a top speed of 120 mph (193 kph).

The 'Father of Streamlining' was the title given to the Paris-born Raymond Loewy, who moved to the United States after the First World War and came to prominence as an industrial designer in the late 1920s. He designed cars, streamlined housings for locomotives, household appliances and – in 1961 – the Studebaker Avanti now coveted by automobile collectors. When designing the Avanti, Loewy said he wanted something that suggested a supersonic aircraft – yet more evidence of the massive influence aviation had on vehicles of all kinds. It was surely no coincidence that in his youth in France, Loewy had won several awards for his model aircraft. During the First World War the styling of aircraft, especially their fuselages, was progressively influenced by the aerodynamic advantages of streamlining. In America some years later, Loewy applied the same principles to a ship, the Virginia Ferry Company's SS *Princess Anne*, whose rakish lines made it look much swifter than it actually was. In this he was possibly influenced by Norman Bel Geddes' model of a proposed streamlined passenger liner.

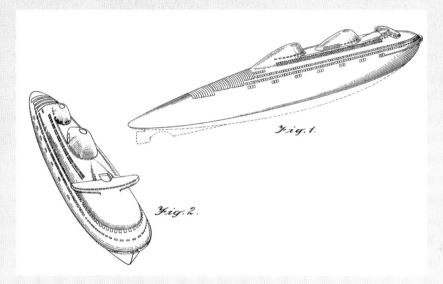

Bel Geddes' Streamlined Ocean Liner: a 1932 concept. Note the overall 'torpedo' shape, the 'teardrop' fairings of its two funnels and the bridge shaped like a wing.

The S.S. *Princess Anne* Ferry Boat Between Kiptopeke Beach and Norfolk, Virginia   21

61690

Raymond Loewy admitted that his streamlined 1933 design for the *Princess Anne* owed less to a desire for better performance than to what was by then a matter of normal modernist styling. The ship was scuppered in Florida in 1993 as an artificial reef.

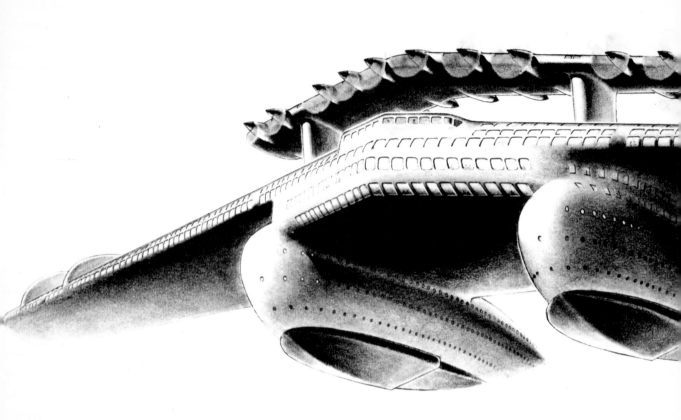

Bel Geddes' futuristic Aircraft No. 4 (1929) was influenced by contemporary 'flying wing' designers like Boris Cheranovsky in the Soviet Union and Jack Northrop in the US. It was perhaps closer to the 'lifting body' principle of the aircraft built by his fellow American, Vincent Burnelli.

Bel Geddes was another industrial (and theatrical) designer of the time, whose 1932 book *Horizons* was highly influential. He left a multitude of models and sketches, many of them quite impracticable and futuristic but showing how well he understood the glamour of speed and modernity. It was he and contemporary designers like him who gave swift, rounded shapes to domestic appliances like refrigerators, cookers, vacuum cleaners and even to humble desktop pencil sharpeners.

Like the Swiss-French architect and urban planner Le Corbusier, Bel Geddes foresaw a future of mass travel in which aircraft would take on the dimensions of ocean-going liners. One of his projects between 1929 and 1932 was for a Transoceanic Passenger Plane, his Aircraft No. 4. This was a behemoth 'flying wing' seaplane with nine decks and a wingspan of 160 metres (525 ft). It was designed for 451 passengers and in Bel Geddes' own words would be 'equal in spaciousness and comfort to the most modern ocean liner'. The main dining room was designed to seat 200 guests, and the crew of 155 included two head waiters, two wine stewards and nine bar stewards – not to mention seven musicians, a masseur, a masseuse,

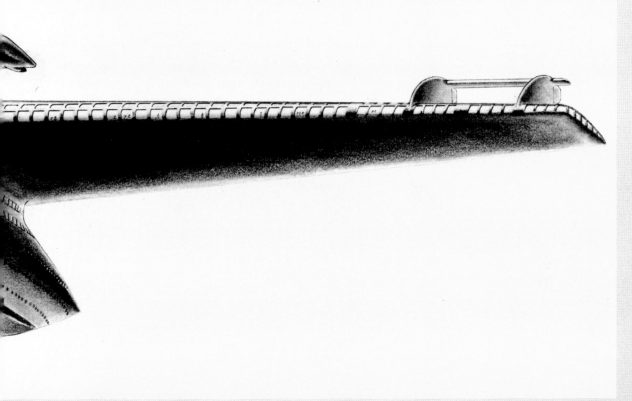

a gymnast and a librarian. He was very much less specific about the mechanics of the thing. In sheer extravagance his Aircraft No. 4 might easily have featured as a typical cover illustration on any contemporary issue of a futuristic monthly magazine like *Modern Mechanics* or Hugo Gernsback's *Air Wonder Stories*. The multitude of burgeoning technologies in the interwar years stimulated vast numbers of imaginative ideas, a few of which were truly prophetic – but most of which were mere science-fiction pipe dreams.

This 'streamline moderne' or 'art moderne' style also greatly influenced the late art deco school of architecture. An important ingredient was the idea of *travel*: the modern and widespread restlessness increasingly made possible by more money, new technologies, and work that depended ever more on attending distant meetings at a client's expense. This architectural style favoured long horizontal lines with curved surfaces and nautical influences such as porthole windows, thus melding the stylish chic of ocean liners with that of gracious living at the best addresses on land. The Pierre Patout building (1935) on Paris's Boulevard Victor is a good instance of *le style paquebot* or 'ocean liner style'. An even more obvious example is the Hotel Normandie in San Juan, Puerto Rico. Obviously designed in honour of the 1935 liner *Normandie* (still judged by many as the epitome of speed and elegance among pre-war transatlantic liners) the hotel is long with a rounded front as if forging through ocean spray. The floors are marked horizontally like decks, with railings and even little 'bridge wing' protrusions at the four corners of the top 'deck'. And as if to show that this style of architecture can still look thoroughly in place and contemporary, especially in a marine context, there is the Van Alen Building on the seafront in Brighton, England. Named in honour of the architect of the sublime art deco masterpiece, the Chrysler Building in New York City, this residential building was finished in 2001. Appropriately, all the apartments have sea views and there are even some porthole windows at the side.

◇◇◇◇◇◇◇◇◇◇◇◇◇◇◇◇◇◇◇◇◇◇

In 1909 the avant-garde Italian poet Filippo Marinetti published his *Manifesto of Futurism*: a hymn to speed, technology and youth. It was a modernist philosophy whose wholesale rejection of anything old (especially politics) challenged established values and promoted a spirit of competitiveness, whether at a personal or national level. In particular, Futurism worshipped

The Hotel Normandie in San Juan, Puerto Rico, opened in 1942 and was deliberately modelled on the SS *Normandie*'s 'streamline moderne' architectural style. The sign on the roof actually came from the ship after a refit.

cars and aircraft for their speed and the beauty deriving from it. (That its praise of youth, power and violence helped it become a central text of Italian fascism is another matter. It was no coincidence that Mussolini, alone among leaders of the major combatants in the Second World War, had bought into this militarism by successfully gaining his pilot's wings.) The spirit of Italian Futurism soon became internationally influential in the new century's art, architecture, industrial design and much else, although the First World War mostly held such things in abeyance until 1920 or so. Even so, the war could be seen as providing other kinds of stimuli. In 1916 Henri Deterding, the chairman of Royal Dutch Shell who was also widely referred to as the 'Napoleon of Oil', predicted, 'This is a century of travel, and the restlessness which has been created by the war will make the desire for travel still greater.'[4]

What is inarguable is that the world's first technological war hastened great advances in machines of all kinds and above all in aircraft, the speed of whose development was quite remarkable. In the summer of 1914 the average military aircraft was of unspecified role other than the all-purpose one of 'observation', since there were as yet no dedicated specialised types such as fighters or bombers. It was typically a fabric-covered wooden-framed biplane with a maximum speed of around 70–80 mph (113–129 kph), a maximum load of two skinny crewmen and an altitude capability of a few thousand feet that could take anything up to three-quarters of an hour to reach. Four years later there were fully aerobatic fighters capable of speeds of 145 mph (233 kph), an ability to climb to 20,000 feet in under twenty minutes and a service ceiling of 25,000 feet. By the end of the war in Europe many people had become accustomed to seeing flying machines; yet the idea of flight remained a marvel – even slightly mystical, which was why aircraft and their pilots acquired a prestige all their own for daring to scoff at the supposed laws of nature. The 'conquest of the air' seemed to most people the greatest marvel of human ingenuity to date, just as fifty years later the conquest of space would be.

The 1920s and 1930s were to be two decades of almost nonstop and highly competitive record-setting in the air, on land and on water. Speed records, altitude records, distance records, endurance records: all were established and broken and re-established by men – and often women – who became household names and public heroes. The thrills of high-speed driving and flying were acknowledged everywhere in books, newspapers, magazines and films. Motorcycles, cars, aircraft, speedboats, transatlantic liners, even trains: all were raced – often as much for glory as for money

T. E. Lawrence's Brough Superior: the last of eight he owned. He never rode this machine as it was being built when he was killed riding No. 7 in May 1935. To this day the marque is known as 'the Rolls-Royce of motorcycles'.

– and the various marques of machines became famous for their beautiful functionality just as their 'speed merchant' drivers did for their blithe habit of dicing with death. Thus T. E. Lawrence (of Arabia), helmetless and muddy on his Brough Superior motorbike, would time-race himself on trips from Dorset to London in all weathers over mostly appalling country roads. Thus also the fictional Simon Templar ('The Saint') drove his (equally fictional) large Hirondel car at breakneck speed through his early adventures to save a heroine – or even civilisation itself – in the nick of time. It was taken for granted that The Saint was also a skilled pilot. In fact, the First World War was scarcely over and the Royal Air Force barely founded before airmen became notorious for their reckless driving of fast cars, so much so that by the 1930s insurance companies had begun imposing a crippling premium on RAF personnel.

And yet mere brute speed on its own was not always enough to make an enviable public statement. There was equal kudos to be gained by the tastefulness and stylishness in which one could now travel. Cars in particular might achieve real elegance without necessarily being the fastest on the market. The pure beauty of expensive engineering became associated with stateliness and grace, as was soon apparent in marques of luxury cars like Rolls-Royce, Mercedes, Bugatti, Hispano-Suiza, Pierce-Arrow, Duesenberg,

Delage and sundry others. In these very expensive automobiles, mechanical excellence, finish and interior detailing were of prime importance.

◇◇◇◇◇◇◇◇◇◇◇◇◇◇◇◇◇◇◇◇◇◇◇◇

If we conclude that the age of speed and elegance was arguably at its most refined between 1900 and late 1941 when the United States entered the Second World War, we must also acknowledge how assiduously it was moulded by films and newsreels of the period. Hollywood's potent images of luxurious cars, trains, liners and aircraft – allied as they so often were with stories of romance and adventure – helped foster the association of speed with glamour and excitement.

The way in which these various modes of travel developed was surprisingly little slowed by the Wall Street Crash of 1929 that led to years of depression and economic downturn – a trend reversed only by rapid rearmament preceding the Second World War. It was a time when it was quite unusual to call technological progress into question (unless you were H. G. Wells), other than maybe to lament the brute mechanisation of war. Above all it was an era when almost no one worried about the environmental consequences of the swift advances in engineering and industry, and certainly not that they might have an impact on a planetary scale. This was long before the shadow of global warming fell across such advances and the change in lifestyles they enabled. To that extent, one could say that the age of speed and elegance was also one of comparative innocence as it blithely overtook its old natural models. It finally left the 80 mph swordfish and the 217 mph peregrine falcon trailing in its wake.

1

SHIPS

n the nineteenth century, Britain, then by far the world's largest and most innovative shipbuilder and with a vast empire to service, maintained the most comprehensive global network of sea routes. From the middle of the century the North Atlantic crossing from western Europe to the US and Canada became the most lucrative and important route. It was a money-earner chiefly because of the huge numbers of migrants flowing from impoverished Europe to a new life in America, but also because of a growing number of bankers, businessmen and entrepreneurs with interests and footholds on both sides of the Atlantic.

The beginning of the 'grand' era of the big ocean liner could arguably be dated from the launch of RMS *Oceanic* in 1870 – the White Star Line's first contender for the route. By today's standards she was small and primitive in that, although steam driven by a single screw, she still carried masts for full sail. This was a fail-safe at a time when mechanical breakdown in the mid-Atlantic might easily prove fatal. The company's recognition that its revenue depended on two kinds of passengers was reflected in their division aboard. On her maiden crossing in 1871 *Oceanic* carried 166 first-class (or 'saloon') passengers and 1,000 third-class (or 'steerage') passengers. Hitherto, steerage passengers had been largely restricted to sailing vessels; the conditions in which they travelled were often scandalous and became the subject of a reform movement. In an unusually advanced measure for those days, *Oceanic*'s steerage was still further segregated, with single men berthed in the bow and married men and women with their families in the stern. Also rare for the time was their standard of accommodation. Steerage was nothing like as comfortable as saloon class, but by the standards of the day it was still considered outstanding. A contemporary report described *Oceanic* as 'more like an imperial yacht',[1] although that might have been the White Star Line talking. Certainly the first-class cabins were equipped with running water and even an electric bell for summoning the steward.

In 1871 the White Star Line's RMS *Oceanic* arguably became the first of the 'great' passenger liners to ply the prestigious transatlantic route. Note the provision of masts for emergency sails.

Four years later the White Star Line's main rival, the Cunard Line, responded with a new ship of its own: RMS *Bothnia*. A second, RMS *Scythia*, was launched in 1875. Both had the first onboard libraries as well as rooms for reading and writing reserved exclusively for the use of female passengers. Each ship could manage a sustained speed of 15 knots, which at just over 17 mph (27 kph) was fast for the day.

An intense rivalry now developed between the White Star, Cunard and Inman lines for this prestigious transatlantic route. Competition was chiefly over speed and passenger comfort, although the matter of safety was never far behind in the minds of either owners or passengers. These 3,000 miles of empty ocean had for centuries been notorious for bad weather and lost ships. Yet the number of passengers was steadily increasing, making speed and reliability paramount to ensure the quickest voyage and turnaround times. The Inman Line's *City of Berlin* (1875) was bigger and faster than any of White Star or Cunard's ships and soon won the unofficial – but commercially important – record for the fastest East–West Atlantic crossing. (The term 'Blue Riband' was not then in use and only became common in the early years of the twentieth century.) By today's standards of massive cruise liners these were small vessels whose best saloon-class accommodation would strike modern seagoers as less than generous. The *City of Berlin* was grand for its day, but still displaced a mere 5,491 tons.

Then in 1881 German competition took a hand with the SS *Elbe*: the Glasgow-built first of Norddeutscher Lloyd's eleven steamships named after rivers. They were intended for speed as well as setting new standards of design. Hitherto, nearly all passenger liners had four decks, the lowest two being for the engines, stores, cargo and crew quarters. Under this arrangement steerage passengers were on the third deck while the fourth or upper deck was reserved for first- (and sometimes second-) class passengers, whose cabins or 'staterooms' typically surrounded the saloon and dining room in the middle of the ship, where the vessel's motion was least noticeable. The *Elbe* and her sister ships added a new upper deck where the first-class saloons were re-sited. Instead of being hemmed in by cabins as previously, these grand rooms now extended to both sides of the ship, creating a new sense of spaciousness while also allowing for a ladies' drawing room and a smoking room for the gentlemen.

From then on, vessels for this primary transatlantic route were increasingly designed as much as possible to make first- and even second-class passengers forget they were on a ship – much less one suspended above black chasms of cold water, often several miles deep, that had claimed so many lives and proud vessels in the previous 500 years and would readily claim theirs, too, if anything went seriously wrong. The liners grew in size even as they grew in comfort.

◇◇◇◇◇◇◇◇◇◇◇◇◇◇◇◇◇◇◇◇◇◇◇◇

It was the ships' increasing size that, as the turn of the twentieth century neared, induced governments to take a hand in what until then had been purely a matter of private enterprise. The principal reason was that both Germany and Britain were rapidly modernising their respective navies while casting nervous glances at each other's progress. One example was the British Admiralty's alarm as it watched its German counterpart designing and building a powerful U-boat fleet. This was at the very moment when elderly but still-influential officers of the Royal Navy could be heard saying that submarines were 'un-British' and 'a dashed underhanded way of waging warfare' and should not be seriously considered. Luckily, younger influences prevailed and Britain followed suit in building submarines. At the same time British and European defence chiefs could see that the latest big transatlantic liners could, in the event of war, become vital assets as troopships, and the bigger and faster the better. They might even be lightly armed if constructed with suitably reinforced places for gun mounts.

Cunard's sister ships *Campania* and *Lucania* (the latter pictured below) were the first transatlantic liners to benefit from government backing – in this case funds from the British Admiralty, whose speediest warships were eclipsed by these far swifter civilian vessels.

The potential of such ships was made plainly evident when the Cunard Line commissioned two new liners in 1891, *Campania* and *Lucania*. They would not only be the heaviest and fastest transatlantic liners to date but would easily outperform the cream of the British navy in both size and speed. When they entered service in 1893 they displaced 18,450 tons apiece, were 189 metres (620 ft) in length and had a service speed of 22 knots (but were theoretically capable of a short burst of 23.5 knots or 27 mph / 43.5 kph). As an indication of how much smaller and slower even the largest of the Royal Navy's capital ships were, in that same year Britain's biggest battleship, HMS *Victoria*, was famously rammed and sunk by another British battleship, HMS *Camperdown*, while on manoeuvres in the Mediterranean. *Victoria* was 100 metres (328 ft) long, displaced 11,200 tons and had a maximum speed of 17.3 knots (19.9 mph / 32 kph). Small wonder the Royal Navy had insisted that the two new Cunarders were built to Admiralty specifications, in return for which they were partly funded by government money.

Engine technology had now reached the stage of rendering auxiliary sails redundant. Both new liners had the world's largest reciprocating engines of the day: gigantic triple expansion engines so tall they occupied the entire depth of the ship, their cylinder heads emerging through the upper deck and requiring a separate deckhouse to cover them. Once in service and achieving the fastest Atlantic crossings, *Campania* and *Lucania* effectively constituted a challenge that was both commercial and military and the Germans were quick to respond. Norddeutscher Lloyd's magnificent twin-screw *Kaiser Wilhelm der Grosse* was launched in 1897 and promptly captured the speed record for the fastest crossing, being half a knot quicker than the Cunarders. Westminster was mortified as well as alarmed. Cunard would also have taken note of the German ship's pioneering design.

SS *Kaiser Wilhelm der Grosse* was the first 'four-stacker'. She and her three sister ships were also the first 'superliners' designed for a new era of luxury travel and also to win the Blue Riband for Germany. This she did in 1897.

For a start, the vessel was the first of the 'four-stackers', having four funnels. From then on, this feature carried a distinct psychological component. The travelling public was quick to associate a ship's number and size of funnels with superior potency, speed and safety, even to the point where ships would often be built with dummy funnels to heighten the effect. (In this respect 'funnel envy' could be said to have borne a faint generic resemblance to the boasted number and size of a nation's ballistic missiles, as we now see well over a century later in the time of Presidents Kim Jong-un and Donald Trump.) Its four funnels apart, the new German vessel's first-class spaces were of unprecedented size and lavishness. They were largely kitted out in a vaguely baroque-revival style calculated to delude travellers into thinking they were really guests in some historic country mansion, open fireplaces and all. The distribution of the ship's classes faithfully reflected the day's commercial realities. Of 1,500-odd passengers, 206 were first class; 226 were second class; while the remaining 1,068 were third class ('steerage' by any other name) and largely provided the crossing's basic revenue.

SS *Kaiser Wilhelm der Grosse*'s First Class smoking room.

Steerage passengers up for a breath of fresh air.

In 1900 *Kaiser Wilhelm der Grosse* also set a new standard by becoming the first ship with radio. At the time, Guglielmo Marconi's early equipment may have been primitive by later standards since it only allowed for transmitting and receiving messages in Morse code; but a dedicated 'Marconi room' added considerably to the ship's aura of safety and modernity. The following year saw Marconi installations in both *Campania* and *Lucania*, staffed by trained wireless officers, and soon a radio range of 3,000 miles was possible. This not only allowed for the shipping lines to follow their own vessels' progress across the Atlantic but also made it possible for business passengers to communicate with their head offices from mid-ocean – and thence by telegraph across America or Europe and around the globe. The lines were quick to spot this as a further source of revenue.

◇◇◇◇◇◇◇◇◇◇◇◇◇◇◇◇◇◇◇◇◇◇◇◇

In the meantime much progress had been made in the technology of ships' engines. The huge triple expansion engines increasingly common in liners like *Lucania* and *Campania* were marvels of Victorian engineering – but they had their drawbacks, not the least of which being the sheer amount of space they occupied. They were reciprocating engines, which meant huge pistons stopping dead at the top and bottom of each stroke. Although this was counterbalanced by the pistons in mid-stroke in neighbouring cylinders, the action inevitably created wear and tear on bearings as well as vibration that was felt all over the ship. Sir Charles Parsons' invention of the steam turbine in 1884 had proved immensely influential. At the Spithead Navy Review of 1897 he cheekily exhibited his little yacht *Turbinia* to immense effect. Nonchalantly running up and down the lines of naval vessels at a fraction under 40 mph (64 kph), it was completely uncatchable by the picket boat vainly chasing after it – as well it might have been, since on that day it was easily the fastest vessel in the world. The steam turbine offered clear advantages in being more compact and far smoother running while promising greater speed for the same amount of coal consumed. It was, in fact, more economical at high speed than it was at low.

What was more, Parsons had also done pioneering work on propellers and the phenomenon of cavitation. Cavitation is caused by a rapidly turning propeller when its speed through the water lowers the pressure along its edges, causing air to come out of solution and form whirling strands and pockets of bubbles that promptly collapse. The split-second implosion of these small air pockets is accompanied by intense heat as well as sonic energy which, although underwater, can easily be transmitted through a steel vessel and was already a recognised source of additional noise aboard the faster liners. It was further discovered that over time the effects of cavitation could eventually erode the propeller itself. The noise made by the collapsing bubbles remains to this day one of the most researched ways of detecting submarines by sonar. Improved propeller design allied to the new generation of steam turbines was to revolutionise the propulsion of liners and warships alike in the first half of the twentieth century.

◇◇◇◇◇◇◇◇◇◇◇◇◇◇◇◇◇◇◇◇◇◇◇◇◇

Cunard, convinced that steam turbines were the engines of the future, commissioned two new ships bigger, grander and more beautiful than any that had gone before. These were RMS *Mauretania* and RMS *Lusitania*. In keeping with prevailing military considerations, their designers modelled the ships' hulls in Royal Navy experimental tanks. The optimum shape turned out to be somewhat narrower than usual. The result was two elegantly slender vessels that, with their speed, were to earn the journalistic description of 'ocean greyhounds'. Both ships were launched in 1906 and after various trials and modifications entered service the following year. *Lusitania* promptly captured the record for the fastest eastbound and westbound Atlantic crossings. Two months later *Mauretania* beat her sister ship's record to gain the eastbound Blue Riband.

Each ship was able to make the transatlantic crossing in about four and a half days. The ideal for Cunard would have been to offer a weekly service with the two vessels crossing in the mid-Atlantic, but logistics made it impossible. Steam was still raised in coal-fired boilers and the disadvantage of coal was that refuelling ('bunkering') was a slow and laborious process. This was further lengthened by the ship needing to be completely sluiced down after bunkering to remove the coating of coal dust that clung to surfaces everywhere. Still, even without being able to keep an ideal schedule, both ships were from the start immensely popular with passengers. Soon it became a matter of some snobbery to choose to travel on the two new Cunarders rather than on White Star vessels which, grand and reliable as they undoubtedly were, suddenly seemed a bit 'old hat' (as Cunard passengers no doubt scoffed in their shipboard letters home).

With their two new flagships, Cunard had made some calculated decisions. The company was convinced that profitability depended on their passengers' shipboard conditions, and above all those in steerage. They were determined to attract as many emigrants as they could for their East–West service since they were the liners' cash cow. Consequently they had designed quarters for steerage passengers that were a great advance on the norm, with decent accommodation in shared cabins, a proper large dining room and even a smoking room and a separate ladies' writing room. This gamble paid off handsomely, with mass transit passengers now actively choosing to cross to the United States on *Lusitania* and *Mauretania* just like their more upmarket fellow passengers.

As for the wealthy, their accommodation and public spaces now scaled new heights of luxury. The two new vessels set a standard that thereafter became common throughout the industry. From now on, the grandest space in a liner was usually the immense first-class dining room, now typically two decks deep and topped with a dome. The new Cunarders had tables for 323 diners on the lower level and 147 on the upper, which effectively became a vast curved balcony. The actual interior decor of these great spaces differed on each ship. On *Lusitania* it was vaguely Louis XIV: all gold leaf, Greek columns, chandeliers and frescoes inside the dome. It was an invocation of grand luxe that eighty years later would readily decay into a style one might call Trump Tower baroque. *Mauretania's* first-class restaurant, on the other hand, was an altogether more sober affair, with rare woods and a wood-pillared balcony for the upper saloon, all topped by a white coffered dome with intricate wood ribbing. This space avoided being oppressive by being beautifully lit with electric light. Both ships had lifts caged in filigreed Edwardian bronze work for their first-class passengers. This was probably the moment when the fashion was finally set for the interior design of transatlantic liners to become extravagantly themed – to reassure first- and even second-class passengers that they were safely cocooned in a cross between the most lavish terrestrial hotel and a country mansion like Syon House. It was, of course, all designed to make money; and this it most successfully did.

Meanwhile, the owners of the White Star Line – hitherto considered to have had a stranglehold on the premium luxury market – were dismayed that their 'big four' ships had been upstaged by their Cunarder rivals even though the last of the White Star four, *Adriatic* (launched in the same month as *Mauretania*), was the first transatlantic liner to offer its first-class passengers a Turkish bath and an indoor swimming pool. Moreover, their 'big four' were a few thousand tons smaller than the Cunarders, and tonnage – like the number of funnels – seemed to play significantly with potential travellers.

The White Star Line's RMS *Adriatic* of 1907 deliberately favoured her passengers' comfort over sheer speed. First-class passengers were increasingly found to favour shipboard amenities over earlier arrival at their destination.

White Star's owners responded by ordering three new liners, each at least half as heavy again as their rivals and more than a hundred feet longer. So big were they that expensive modifications were needed at Harland & Wolff's shipyard before the ships' keels could even be laid, and the White Star pier in New York had also to be lengthened. (Sixty years later, similar expensive modifications had to be made at major airports the world over in order to accommodate Boeing's new 747 'Jumbo' jets when they began operations in 1970, and then again when the Airbus A380 entered service in 2007. Such are the hidden costs in the race for economies of scale.)

Cunard's *Lusitania* and *Mauretania*, both launched in 1906, were the fastest liners of their day. *Lusitania* (shown below) was torpedoed in 1915 for carrying armaments: a fact successive British governments lied about until her wreck was dived on in the 1980s and it was found to be true.

The White Star Line's projected monsters were known as the 'Olympic class' ships – named after the first of the ships, launched in 1911 – and the names of all three were to have connections with Greek mythology: *Olympic*, *Titanic* and *Gigantic*. Each was to be a four-stacker (including one dummy funnel for appearances), 268 metres (880 ft) in length and weighing over 45,000 tons; by Edwardian standards, almost unimaginably huge and at the time certainly the largest-ever manmade moving objects. Each had nine passenger decks (two more than the Cunard Line's *Mauretania* and *Lusitania*). From the boat deck, first-class passengers descended into their richly layered realm below via a grand staircase beneath a wrought-iron and glass dome, in which hung a vast crystal chandelier. Also on the upper deck was a gym with exercise cycles, rowing machines and wall bars – a facility that then seemed an amazing shipboard novelty. Since the new Olympic class liners were so much more spacious, large areas could be given up to lounges and other facilities for all classes.

Olympic in 1911 and *Titanic* in 1912 were two of a projected trio of White Star liners (*Gigantic* was never built). This is the staircase from *Olympic* copied for the 1997 film *Titanic*.

In June 1911 *Olympic*'s maiden voyage to New York and back attracted intense newspaper coverage. It was a stupendous success, with both press and public overawed by her sheer size and the spaciousness for all classes. The crossings were fast, if not quite of Blue Riband standard, for the White Star board had never intended the Olympic class ships to be quite as fast as their Cunard rivals. Instead of being greyhounds of the ocean they would be more like serenely progressing Ritz Hotels, the last word in passengers' red carpet treatment. Comfort and safety were now seen as paramount, including for the immigrants in third class who now shared many of the second-class passengers' spaces. Certainly the degree to which *Olympic*'s successful maiden two-way trip was trumpeted by the press on both sides of the Atlantic was extreme. Indeed, a sceptic might have wondered whether the connection of the ships' names to Greek mythology meant that hubris could be awaiting condign punishment, too much self-congratulation on the part of White Star perhaps meriting a spectacular fall.

Titanic remains notorious for her doomed maiden voyage. Her and *Olympic*'s vast size was matched by the grandeur of the ships' interior design.

By April 1912 *Olympic*'s sister ship *Titanic* was ready for her own maiden voyage. Since the extravaganzas that had greeted *Olympic* the previous year, press interest had cooled somewhat and *Titanic*'s debut was treated as a rather more humdrum event, people by now having grown accustomed to the sheer size and luxury of the new White Star liners. The fate that befell *Titanic* as she neared Newfoundland on her very first crossing is too well known to bear repetition here. Suffice it to say that only 705 of her over 2,200 passengers and crew survived. After various inquests the British Board of Trade was deemed to have failed to keep up with the new ships' sheer size, licensing them to sail with far too few lifeboats for the number of people aboard. White Star's designers, too, were equally to blame for the lack of lifeboats, having relied too much on their vessels' supposed 'unsinkability'. Their 'watertight' compartments had turned out to be not high enough to prevent progressive flooding as the vessel's list in the water increased. Bluntly put, in the rush to get them launched, *Titanic* and *Olympic* had entered service with fundamental design flaws. Such has been a familiar enough story with new technology the world over, often with tragic results. Some forty years later, Britain's de Havilland Comet would be rushed into the air in order to be the world's first fully pressurised jet airliner in service when, in the words of a test pilot who had flown it, it was 'nothing like a hundred per cent aeroplane'.[2] But, as with *Titanic*, independent technical input would doubtless have been resisted on grounds of company pride as well as a fear of permitting outsiders to glimpse trade secrets. Even so, the Olympic class designs must certainly have had Admiralty scrutiny at some point; yet even that failed to pick up the defects.

One result of the loss of the *Titanic* was that White Star renamed their projected third new liner *Britannic* instead of *Gigantic*. Following the sinking, *Oceanic* was quickly withdrawn and refitted not only with lifeboat capacity for the entire ship's complement but also with vertical extensions to its bulkheads and a double-skinned hull for the engine room. *Britannic*'s construction included these safety modifications as a matter of course.

◇◇◇◇◇◇◇◇◇◇◇◇◇◇◇◇◇◇◇◇◇◇◇

It is most unlikely that anyone in the Cunard Line's boardroom greeted the tragedy that afflicted their deadly rivals with anything other than a heartfelt 'There, but for the grace of God…', since they well understood the risks of the business they shared. In any case, within three years their

Opposite: *Olympic*'s maiden voyage in 1911 was rapturously greeted on both sides of the Atlantic as promising the last word in comfort and spaciousness for all three classes of transatlantic passengers.

own glamorous *Lusitania* would also be lost in a sinking that at the time was of equal notoriety to that of *Titanic*. On this occasion the international consequences were far wider since by then the First World War was in its second year. In May 1915, on an eastbound crossing to Liverpool from New York, *Lusitania* was torpedoed by a German U-boat eleven miles off Ireland. Out of 1,962 passengers and crew aboard, only 764 survived. This act of war against a passenger liner caused global outrage. The innocence of a shipload of civilians falling victim to 'German beastliness' was played up in newspapers all over the British empire and the United States. Indeed, because there were so many American victims the incident is widely believed to have hastened the United States' eventual decision to join the Allied war effort against Germany.

In retrospect, however, matters were nothing like so clear-cut. For a start, the Germans knew perfectly well that, like their own passenger liners, the big British ships had all been designed under close military scrutiny in case they should be later required as troopships. They could also easily be converted to armed merchant cruisers – *Lusitania* had been built with gun mounts already in place although no weapons had yet been fitted. Before her fatal return crossing, the German embassy in New York had urged German subjects not to travel because the liner was now considered a legitimate target. The British not only classed and officially listed her as an auxiliary cruiser, but despite the pretence of being an entirely civilian vessel she was known to be carrying munitions. The German embassy even put large posters on the Cunard pier warning all passengers that at the end of the voyage *Lusitania* would be sailing into British waters and hence into a recognised war zone where vessels flying an Allied flag would be liable to search or attack. (Barely thirty years later there would be a Cold War parallel when Berlin was in Soviet-controlled East Germany and all flights to West Berlin were along three air 'corridors'. Flight plans were filed in advance by the Allied-run Berlin Air Safety Centre and cleared by East Germany with the warning stamp 'Safety of Flight Not Guaranteed'.) It is unknown how many of *Lusitania*'s potential passengers were deterred in 1915. The sheer size of the ship, and her aura of invincible modern engineering and civilised comfort, probably reassured most people. And besides, it was surely patriotic to refuse to be cowed.

Nonetheless, *Lusitania* was indeed carrying a military cargo, the details of which appeared on her manifest and were published by the *New York Times* the day after she was sunk. In her hold she had well over four million rounds of small arms ammunition and 1,248 live 3-inch shells boxed in cases that together weighed 50 tons. Despite these facts having been made public by a trusted American newspaper, for nearly seventy years successive British governments carried on with their flat denial that the vessel had been carrying munitions. Only in the early 1980s, when recreational divers began finding burst crates of ammunition in the wreck, was an official warning published that *Lusitania*'s cargo might be dangerously unstable. Back in 1915 German propagandists – excusably in full 'We did warn you' mode – produced a popular iron commemorative medal of the sinking. On one side there was a bas relief of the ship going down with munitions spilling off her foredeck and the words 'No Contraband Goods!' in German. On the medal's obverse passengers were depicted lining up at a Cunard Line ticket office being handed their tickets by a skeleton. In the background the top-hatted German ambassador can be seen raising an admonishing finger as one of the passengers reads a poster announcing 'U-boat Danger'. The heavily ironic slogan on this side of the medal is 'Business Above All'. Had the positions been reversed one can hardly doubt that British propaganda would have made an equal meal of it.

In the last years of peace before the First World War, the two main German lines, Norddeutscher Lloyd and Hamburg-Amerika, had found themselves trailing in the transatlantic stakes. Cunard's *Lusitania* and *Mauretania* had them beaten for speed and White Star's Olympic class liners outdid them in design and luxury. Consequently they planned three new giant liners of over 50,000 tons that would also be the first to be over 275 metres (900 ft) long. The first of these was SS *Imperator*, thus named at Kaiser Wilhelm's insistence, her sister ships being SS *Vaterland* and SS *Bismarck*. It was a matter of German national pride that on her maiden voyage in June 1913 *Imperator* was 7.3 metres (24 ft) longer than *Titanic* had been. Moreover her construction was safer, being double-hulled from the start. Lessons had been learned from *Titanic*'s celebrated fate.

But Cunard was also working on a third liner after *Lusitania* and *Mauretania*. This was *Aquitania*, and while she was being built, her overall length was a closely guarded secret. On the day before Hamburg-Amerika's launch of their new flagship, Cunard announced that *Aquitania* would be one foot longer than *Imperator*. However, the wily German line was no stranger to competition. Having foreseen that Cunard might well pull a last-minute trick to upstage their vessel, Hamburg-Amerika had commissioned a Berlin sculptor to make a large Imperial eagle which now, bolted on the ship's prow as a figurehead, made *Imperator* once again the world's longest ship by a couple of feet. Size matters.

Nor did *Imperator* and its two sister ships disappoint in terms of onboard luxury, which surpassed even that offered by *Mauretania* and *Oceanic*. Yet it was soon revealed that the hurriedly launched German ship had her own serious shortcomings. The sheer weight of *Imperator's* upper decks with their tons of first-class extravagance – plush carpets, heavy beds and furniture, en-suite bathrooms and marble pillars, the now-obligatory bronze lift cages, swimming- and Turkish baths, not to mention the redundant fourth funnel – made her top-heavy and unstable, especially when turning. In short, by no means seaworthy for the potentially stormy North Atlantic. Moreover, her fourth-class accommodation for migrant passengers was definitely inferior to that offered by both Cunard and White Star. *Imperator* was quickly returned to her builders for extensive modification and refitting.

By now a major change to big liners of the era was under way. Coal was being replaced by oil. This was logical on all counts. Oil was cleaner and, being more energy-efficient than coal, its storage aboard took up far less space. It also made bunkering quicker with no need to wash down the decks and superstructure afterwards, which greatly improved turnaround times in port. No longer were up to 200 stokers required to labour away in the stifling and filthy bowels of the ship, shovelling coal into the blazing maws of several dozen boilers as, 50 feet above them, passengers were served quails in aspic and champagne beneath a many-splendoured dome. This change put stokers out of work and eventually also whole communities ashore who were dependent on coal-related trades; but it meant immediate economic advantage to the shipping lines. The last big coal-burning liners were *Aquitania* and *Vaterland*, both launched in 1913. The slightly older *Mauretania* and *Olympic* were converted to oil burning between 1919 and 1920.

As had been foreseen, once hostilities had broken out in the First World War, *Mauretania*, *Aquitania* and *Olympic* were immediately requisitioned for war service, initially as armed merchant cruisers. What had not been foreseen, however, was soon learned the hard way: that enormous liners designed as greyhounds of the ocean were completely unsuited to the abrupt requirements of wartime manoeuvres and ad hoc port facilities. Not only were they too big to make nimble course changes but they were above all wildly uneconomical, consuming great quantities of fuel that the designers had assumed would be replenished every four or five days at

whichever port they reached. Having failed as armed cruisers the vessels mainly became troopships, while the third Olympic class liner, *Britannic*, became a hospital ship and sank off the coast of Greece in November 1916 following an explosion believed to have been caused by a mine.

Whether as troopships or hospitals, however, the great liners were very effective. Never before had armies been able to move so many men with so much materiel so far or so quickly. To that extent it can be said that the steamship lines played a part in changing the nature of warfare. The great German liners also had this role thrust upon them, but unfortunately for some of them they turned out to be on the wrong side. When the outbreak of war caught several in the mid-Atlantic they elected to make a run for New York to take shelter in the then-neutral United States. These included SS *Vaterland*, *Kaiser Wilhelm II* and *Kronprinz Wilhelm*. However, once America had belatedly declared war in April 1917 *Vaterland* was summarily turned over to the US navy, who renamed her SS *Leviathan*. After the war she reverted to being a liner, but now under the flag of the United States Lines. The two Kaiser class liners impounded in the US served as troopships.

White Star's *Majestic* was originally Hamburg-Amerika's *Bismarck* (*Imperator*'s sister ship). In 1919 she was handed over to the White Star Line as part of war reparations and was re-named *Majestic*. This was *Bismarck*'s and *Majestic*'s sumptuous Roman-style swimming bath.

In the United Kingdom, *Vaterland*'s sister ship SS *Bismarck* was taken over by the White Star Line as part of reparations and renamed RMS *Majestic*.

Once peace had been declared the surviving great liners were swiftly refitted to new standards of opulence. With their newly efficient oil-fed boilers they were soon back in business on the transatlantic run. But the world had changed; and before long some new economic and social factors began to threaten the companies' profitability. The first of these was America's Emergency Immigration Act of 1921. This put a cap on unrestricted immigration and began a quota system for European and other migrants. In the immediate aftermath of war, unemployment in the US had led to considerable popular resentment of immigrants. Three years later came another act further restricting immigrants not only from eastern Europe but also from the Middle East, India and the Far East. The effect on the transatlantic passenger liners was immediate, since their ships had been designed specifically for the steerage trade to make them profitable.

In addition, most European economies – and especially those of Britain, France and Germany – had been devastated by more than four years of war, and fewer potential passengers could afford the expense of transatlantic travel. Britain still had the world's biggest fleet of merchant and passenger ships, but their priorities lay in ensuring cargoes and maintaining administrative and military contact with the far-flung empire as much as with the New World. By contrast the US was the clear economic beneficiary of the war and the early 1920s saw the American middle class acquire a good deal more spending power. It soon emerged that there was a big potential market of increasingly wealthy Americans who for one reason or another wanted to see the world. Passenger lines like Cunard and White Star looked for ways of taking advantage of this by diversifying from their rigid pre-war transatlantic timetable.

◇◇◇◇◇◇◇◇◇◇◇◇◇◇◇◇◇◇◇◇◇◇◇

Back in the late Victorian and Edwardian eras the idea of ship-borne tourism and pleasure cruises in comparatively small vessels had caught on for a select few in Europe. The first cruise is commonly believed to have been that of the British P&O Line ship *Ceylon* when in 1858 she visited Venice and other Mediterranean ports only two years after the end of the Crimean War. She carried a few tens of passengers who with good reason would have considered themselves intrepid. By modern standards conditions were rough both onboard and in the ports they visited. But in those days

Opposite: Cunard's *Aquitania,* launched in 1913, was the last big British coal-burning liner. From now on, the future was oil. But within months of her entering service war broke out and *Aquitania* was requisitioned as probably the world's fastest troopship. This cutaway illustration shows her in her restored, post-war guise as an oil-burner.

travellers everywhere were far hardier and accustomed to slow journeys by coach and horses over unmetalled roads that could be bogs in winter and chokingly dusty in summer. Later in the century cruises by the Hamburg-Amerika Line explored the Norwegian fjords as well as the Mediterranean. After that, cruising for pleasure in passenger steamers (as opposed to private yachts) was a low-key affair commercially speaking, and naturally vanished entirely for the duration of the First World War. But now in the early 1920s the new American market for pleasure cruises looked like being a potential saviour for the big liners built for the transatlantic route.

Initially, Thomas Cook's fashionable pre-war destinations still cast their allure for wealthy American tourists, most of whose ancestors were of European origin. Visiting classical sites in the Mediterranean, the cradles of Western civilisation, the glories of Rome and Renaissance Italy; seeing the Alps and maybe even skiing or climbing them: all had considerable appeal. And of course there was France too, above all famous for wine… Wine! In January 1919 the Volstead Act had come into force in the United States, and making, importing and distributing alcoholic drinks were all prohibited. Suddenly, several weeks on a European liner looked like a reprieve as well as a holiday. Since US vessels were now dry by law the ship would need to be foreign-registered. Indeed, before long, ships of a dozen different flags were operating legitimate short 'booze cruises' out of US ports. Prohibition was a godsend not only to gangsters but to European and other steamship lines as well, and it was they that most benefited from providing American passengers with a cultural alibi.

Better still, with the drop in the number of their transatlantic passengers, especially in the 'off season' of the often stormy winter months, the major companies were only too happy to turn to an even wealthier market. They began a refit of their vessels, converting 'steerage' into a much more comfortable 'tourist' class. They did this by seriously reducing the number of passengers, meaning that previously small cabins could be greatly enlarged into bedrooms with proper beds rather than bunks. With fewer but richer passengers ticket prices could be increased to make up the difference. In this way the remaining great pre-war transatlantic liners were converted into something more dual-purpose. Well able to return to the summer North Atlantic trade as required, they could equally well function as luxury cruise ships for the well-heeled keen to avoid winter and the Volstead Act. The vessels were set-dressed to suit their new role, the heaviest of their pre-war decor being lightened to produce something more redolent of a holiday atmosphere. The ships now had several bars scattered democratically among the decks. This sort of facelift worked for all the major existing liners, except

for the erstwhile *Vaterland* (since renamed *Leviathan*), which was now US-registered and dry. She alone failed to make transatlantic journeys profitable and required a government subsidy. But Cunard's great pre-war liners like *Mauretania* and *Aquitania* were soon kitted out as floating hotels for spending weeks drifting at a leisurely pace around the Mediterranean or Caribbean. In the absence of steerage passengers, the prices of these tours were very high, but the tourists were waited on hand and foot since they were a few hundred enjoying the attention of up to a thousand crew members. Many of the richer passengers would also have brought their own personal servants.

But it was not only the major transatlantic lines that saw the potential for cruises. Royal Mail Lines had taken a gamble by converting RMS *Arcadian* to an all-first-class cruise ship for 350 passengers. *Arcadian* was not a new ship, having been built in 1908 – a 12,000-tonner capable of an unremarkable 16.5 knots (19 mph / 30.6 kph) that had chiefly plied passenger routes to Central and South America. But in 1923 she left Southampton on her first cruise and was an immediate hit. Royal Mail Lines soon found that cruising was actually more profitable than the pre-war South American routes their ships

In the 1920s, Royal Mail Line's *Arcadian* – dating from 1908 – was refitted for Mediterranean cruises. Her swimming pool (somewhat primitive by today's standards) looks as though it was converted from a former hold, but was clearly giving pleasure.

Previous spread: These posters perfectly express the new market for cruises in the inter-war years. Gone is the emphasis on speed and Blue Riband competitiveness. Now the ship's anchor chain and the lazy upward drift of smoke from her single funnel suggest the luxury of dawdling amid sunlit landscapes.

were designed to serve. Following *Arcadian*'s success, several of her fleet companions were likewise converted from three-class liners into first-class cruisers with barber shops and cinemas and outstanding cuisine. Perhaps the most notable of these was *Atlantis*, her pre-war persona as *Andes* having been transformed into a kind of seagoing fun palace. Diverting events were held, such as competitions, pirate nights and masquerade balls, plus of course the inevitable nightly deck dances beneath tropic skies ablaze with unfamiliar constellations. After her 1930 maiden voyage in her new guise, *Atlantis* became arguably the most popular and patronised of all British cruise ships before war once again put a stop to such frivolity.

All this resulted in some fundamental shifts in ship design. In 1921 France's Compagnie Générale Transatlantique had brought into service a new liner, SS *Paris*, whose construction had been delayed by the war. In terms of interior decor she was something of a compromise between the old and the new, with the traditional pre-war baroquery now intriguingly mixed with flashes of art nouveau and even art deco styles. *Paris* also broke new ground by being the first ship to offer her first-class passengers square windows to look out of instead of the usual circular portholes, thereby further helping to banish the sensation of being at sea. The ship was a great success, but even she was eclipsed by the same company's liner that followed her in 1927.

The SS *Île de France* remains one of the few contenders for the title of most beautiful liner of all time. Not only was she externally a work of art but internally she abruptly broke with established tradition by completely renouncing neo-Tudor palace architecture. In its place was a new style that owed much to the pavilions of the Exposition Internationale des Arts Décoratifs et Industriels Modernes that had opened in Paris in 1924. The *Île de France* introduced an art deco style that had roots in art nouveau but which now incorporated the aesthetics of modernism. Lalique glass was reflected in polished black floors. By chance the Wall Street Crash two years after the ship's launch, plus the Great Depression that followed, would help endow this style of decor with a degree of optimism, as if an uncluttered, even light-hearted, modernist future might plausibly lie on the far side of the grim economic downturn that beggared millions and would soon seem endless. But the guests aboard the *Île* (as she was soon known) were insulated in their palace of pleasure, relishing what was internationally recognised as the best cuisine afloat.

This page and next:
In 1927 the *Île de France* amazed transatlantic passengers as much with her interior decor as with her external lines. Something of the flamboyant spirit of modern cruise ships seemed to have influenced her designers, while her cuisine represented the *ne plus ultra* of seaborne gourmandising.

611. LE HAVRE. Le Paquebot "ILE-DE-FRANCE"
Long. 241 m., larg. 28 m., tirant d'eau 9 m. 75.
jauge brute 43.500 tonnes, force 52.000 chevaux, vitesse 23 nœuds,
équipage 800 hommes, 1.200 passagers de 1re et 2e classes,
600 passagers de 3e classe.

S. S. ILE de FRANCE   THE GRAND SALON—SUMPTUOUS—MAGNIFICENT
First Class

In the meantime a different kind of cruise was becoming popular for those with money, unlimited time on their hands and a yen for shipboard luxury. This was the world cruise. In November 1922 Cunard's *Laconia* left New York and would not return for twenty-two weeks, starting a fashion that lasted until 1939 and the outbreak of another world war. William H. Miller, the author of *Sailing to the Sun*, quotes a 1931 magazine advertisement for next winter's world cruise on Cunard's *Franconia*:

Faraway, glamorous places have stirred your imagination! Bali, still in its primitive civilisation; Macassar, flaming like a ruby on the jungle's edge; Bangkok's regal splendour; and Saigon, remote and so special. The Franconia *includes them without extra cost… and all the other highlights of a round-the-world voyage. One-hundred-and-forty days, 33 ports of call and all at greatly reduced rates, beginning at $1,750.*

Note the phrase 'beginning at'; then as now there was scarcely a limit to how much a cruise could actually cost above a basic quoted price. Much depended on how much one drank, the shore excursions, the cuisine of choice and 'extras' among sundry shipboard amenities and diversions as well as (these days) Internet access.

By the early 1930s world cruising was an accepted pastime for the leisured class. All sorts of authors, impresarios and film stars (H. L. Mencken, Noël Coward, Douglas Fairbanks) often spent months at sea, and a good many books, film scripts and popular songs resulted. P. G. Wodehouse, who from Edwardian days had acquired close New York magazine connections even before he went to Hollywood to write film scripts, made frequent transatlantic crossings for professional reasons while remaining disinclined to longer voyages. (His novel *The Luck of the Bodkins* [1935], is almost entirely set aboard the fictitious RMS *Atlantic*.) To judge from references in his books he did not greatly enjoy shipboard life or the company of his fellow travellers. Regardless of the supposedly palatial comfort of first-class travel, his fictional character Bertie Wooster more than once complained about the 'ungodly hour' of the morning at which passengers were obliged to disembark in New York. In one novel Bertie's manservant and helpmeet, Jeeves, is particularly anxious to go on a round-the-world cruise but Bertie hates the idea of being cooped up for weeks on end with the same people, quite apart from 'the nuisance of having to visit the Taj Mahal'. This was clearly his author's own view. Inevitably, though, by the end of the book Bertie has to let Jeeves get his way in exchange for a closely guarded secret Bertie is desperate to know. Unfortunately, we never learn how the cruise went. Bertie would simply have been one of the millionaire passengers who brought their own 'gentleman's personal gentlemen' with them aboard Cunarders like *Franconia* and *Carinthia* or Canadian Pacific's magnificent *Empress of Britain*. On the latter ship he could even have played

---

*In terms of buying power this is roughly equivalent to $30,000 today.

Canadian Pacific's *Empress of Britain* offered all manner of glamorous pastimes to its millionaire passengers, as well as the opportunity to visit some of the touristic wonders of the world.

tennis on the top deck court. Thereafter it would be 30,000 sea miles of card games, deck quoits, flappers, shipboard romance, stuffy cabins, after-dinner entertainments, whiskies-and-sodas and the bore of periodically being rousted out to go and look at the Leaning Tower of Pisa or the Pyramids.

Such a cruise would have left New York, crossed the Atlantic, and thence proceeded via the Mediterranean and the Suez Canal to India. After that would come those alluring Southeast Asian destinations touted by the brochure, then on to Hong Kong, Shanghai and Tokyo before crossing the Pacific via Honolulu and finally through the Panama Canal back to New

York. Bertie Wooster's shipboard suite of rooms would alone have cost him a minimum of $16,000, plus a surcharge for Jeeves of $1,750 (together representing somewhere near a quarter of a million dollars at today's rates). And that was just the start.

⬦⬦⬦⬦⬦⬦⬦⬦⬦⬦⬦⬦⬦⬦⬦⬦⬦⬦⬦⬦⬦

Despite the popularity of ships like *Atlantis* and *Empress of Britain* a good deal of affection still clung to the great pre-war liners like *Mauretania*. Their interior decor might have been updated here and there, but they each retained a loyal following of passengers who refused to travel on any other ship, some even insisting on the same steward. By the early 1930s, however, these liners were getting a little long in the tooth. Painting *Mauretania*'s hull white in 1933 and sending her on short cruises couldn't disguise the fact that she had been launched in 1906 in a long-ago Edwardian era on the other side of a war that had changed the world irrevocably. Depression or no Depression, there were still thousands of business travellers like P. G. Wodehouse who needed to cross the Atlantic as quickly as possible.

The shipping companies' directors would have been well aware of the recent swift advances made by aviation, with long distance and speed records constantly broken and regular passenger services now being flown in Europe and the US. The more astute would have guessed it was only a matter of time before aircraft had improved enough to make transatlantic passenger flights a real possibility instead of intrepid feats by lone aviators. In the early 1930s that moment had not yet arrived, no commercial aircraft having the required range and safety margin while carrying a payload. (It would take the Second World War to stimulate the necessary advances in aero technology.) But the *Graf Zeppelin*'s triumphant 1929 round-the-world flight in twelve flying days with twenty passengers and forty-one crew had spectacularly proved that such flights were not at all in the realm of fiction, at least for dirigibles. Even so, it was still hard to imagine how aircraft could ever become the workhorses of speedy long-distance mass travel. In the meantime, therefore, the transatlantic shipping lines reasoned that a new generation of ocean greyhounds was needed. The White Star and Cunard lines in particular also acknowledged privately that France's superb *Île de France* had already set new standards of design.

With the increasing ideological tensions of the 1930s the transatlantic liner trade, that so recently had been a simple matter of competing private shipping lines, had gradually morphed via international rivalry into a politicised issue involving national supremacy. The White Star Line's projected new ship, RMS *Oceanic*, embodied new thinking in that, from the first, she was expressly designed to regain the Blue Riband. This broke with the company tradition of opting for passenger comfort over sheer speed. The plan also called for a new system of propulsion. More than forty diesel generators would supply electricity to power huge electric motors driving four propellers. In Germany, Norddeutscher Lloyd was also planning two big new Blue Riband contenders, SS *Bremen* and SS *Europa*. The hulls of both these ships incorporated a new idea to increase a vessel's speed. Hydrodynamic experiments had showed that a bulbous protrusion on the bow below the waterline would ease a hull's passage through the water. At the same time this rounded excrescence helped dampen the effects of pitching, leading to a ship that was both swifter and more stable. It was a breakthrough in hull design that was quickly adopted and is more or less ubiquitous today. *Bremen* and *Europa* were both launched in 1928 but *Europa*'s completion was delayed by a fire. On her maiden voyage *Bremen* beat *Mauretania*'s long-standing westward Blue Riband record speed by almost a knot and then on the eastward crossing did slightly better still, becoming the first ship to get a double Blue Riband. When *Europa* entered service in 1930 she promptly took *Bremen*'s record away from her. This German advance made the White Star Line's challenge even more urgent.

However, the sudden drop in transatlantic passengers following the 1929 stock market crash and the ensuing Depression was having a profound effect on the business. It immediately affected the construction of White Star's *Oceanic*, work on the hull having to be suspended in December 1931 when the John Brown Shipyard on Clydebank temporarily laid off workers. *Oceanic* was in fact doomed, and her rusted unfinished hull was later broken up, the steel going to build two smaller ships, MS *Britannic* and MS *Georgic*. These might have been less ambitious in terms of size and speed, but they did retain *Oceanic*'s planned system of diesel-electric propulsion, thereby becoming the world's biggest motor ships.

In Italy Mussolini was determined that an Italian liner would win the coveted Blue Riband, thus showing the world that only fascism could fulfil the predictions of Futurism by fully embracing a machine world. This was probably half true, since Mussolini had amalgamated and nationalised all of Italy's shipping lines and any new liner would be built at government behest and expense. The result was two ships, SS *Rex* and SS *Conte di Savoia* launched in 1931 and 1932 respectively. For all the *Île de France*'s modernist innovations, the new Italian liners were sleek externally but comparatively traditional inside. In August 1933 *Rex* did indeed gain the Blue Riband, her crossing being achieved in four days and thirteen hours at an average speed of nearly 29 knots (33.4 mph / 53.7 kph). Her sister ship, *Conte di Savoia*, was not quite as fast but made up for it by becoming famous as the most stable ship of all time. She achieved this thanks to three enormous gyroscopes mounted in the bows that together considerably dampened the ship's motion. This was widely hailed as a triumph of scientific thinking and the liner at once became immensely popular. Her extravagant Salone Colonna (modelled on Rome's Palazzo Colonna) certainly helped. Between them, these two new Italian ships made inroads into the transatlantic trade.

The SS *Conte di Savoia* was built at Italian government expense as Mussolini's attempt to win Italy a Blue Riband. She never managed this but did gain a reputation as the most stable liner of all time, thanks to three huge gyroscopes mounted in her bows.

However, the French were also busy and the hull of the *Île*'s successor had already been laid when the news came of the White Star Line cancelling and scrapping what existed of *Oceanic*. The Compagnie Générale Transatlantique's cash flow was also in a parlous state and it appealed for government backing. As in the case of Italy, the project was presented as being essential for maintaining the country's reputation and public money was soon found. The result was the SS *Normandie*, launched in October 1932. It was soon clear there had never been a ship like her, not even the beautiful *Île*. Not only was her hull the largest ever constructed but both it and the superstructure were of radical, even streamlined design. The engines were turbo-electric, of proven reliability. But it was her interior that, at a stroke, exceeded the glories of all other liners.

The style was art deco wedded to what would become known as 'streamline moderne' when it caught on as The Look in American industrial design from the early 1930s. In *Normandie* the influence of cruise ships was evident in that first-class accommodation was heavily favoured, its centrepiece being the famous Grand Saloon restaurant, the biggest room in any ship to date, over 93 metres (305 ft) long. Modelled on Versailles' Hall of Mirrors and flanked by twelve Lalique glass pillars it could seat 700 diners at once. The very best of the first-class accommodation was designed to exceed that of any terrestrial hotel. Each of the two major suites comprised several bedrooms, a private dining room, a lounge with a grand piano and, of course, a private external deck screened from the sight of any other passenger. The entire vessel set a completely new standard for shipborne living. It also constituted an outrageous act of sheer chutzpah to produce this enormous and vastly expensive gem of maritime art at a time when both sides of the Atlantic were mired in the Depression.

Normandie's maiden voyage in May 1935 also set a new record. With an average speed of a shade under 30 knots (34.5 mph / 55.6 kph), she captured the Blue Riband and *la gloire* now belonged to France rather than to Italy. But despite all the extravagance, she was never a great commercial success. Maybe after all the luxe was too grand, even intimidatingly so. To this day, and however debatably, she is nevertheless usually remembered as the most beautiful transatlantic passenger liner ever built. This encomium is inevitably tinged with sadness because her life was so short, and her end tragic. As with the German liners in the First World War, *Normandie* was impounded in New York after the fall of France in May 1940 and in due course renamed *Lafayette* and turned into a troopship. Her marvellous interiors were unceremoniously stripped out, with much crashing of Lalique

Opposite: The SS *Normandie* was visually the most beautiful liner of all, both in and out; but like so many beauties she was doomed to a short life and a tragic fate. In 1940, punitively declared an enemy alien by the still-neutral US, she was gutted for a brief career as a troopship.

glass. Then in early 1942 fire broke out on the ship and so much water was pumped in by firemen that she capsized and remained lying on her side, half exposed on the bed of the Hudson River for the rest of the war. She was eventually broken up in 1946.

◇◇◇◇◇◇◇◇◇◇◇◇◇◇◇◇◇◇◇◇◇◇◇◇

Britain had now been bested on the North Atlantic route by Germany, Italy and France, all countries in which powerful nationalistic arguments had triumphed, while cash-strapped shipyards had appealed to their governments for financial backing in order to regain national honour. It was now Britain's turn. The Cunard and White Star lines were merged in a 60–40 per cent deal, Cunard holding the lion's share. With much public rejoicing the John Brown Shipyard went back to work on a new grand liner to challenge the foreign competition. This was the RMS *Queen Mary*, which was launched in the autumn of 1934 and christened by her namesake in person. She was an elegant ship, but very much more traditional than *Normandie*, both inside and out. Her upper deck was still cluttered by large air scoops and she lacked the French ship's streamlined profile. Inside, too, her design broke no radical new ground, opting for the safe art deco style that had now become common in liners. In this careful restraint with more than a hint of tradition, she was emphatically built to British rather than to French tastes and in due course it paid off. Her design naturally incorporated all the amenities that passengers had now grown to expect: shops, two swimming pools (for first and tourist class), libraries, a beauty salon, even (a first for a liner) a synagogue as well as a chapel. Against a background of the Nazi accession to power in Germany the previous year, this was undoubtedly a way of making it clear that Jewish passengers were welcome. Once fitted out and in service, with her generally understated and friendly atmosphere, the *Queen Mary* was an immediate success. Not that she wasn't also a greyhound, even if disguised as a Labrador. In August 1936 she won back the Blue Riband for Britain, triggering considerable jubilation at home and especially on Clydebank.

The quest for speed supremacy was by no means over, however, and *Normandie* soon made a rival bid and won back the Blue Riband in 1937. A year later *Queen Mary* regained it with a crossing in three days, twenty-one hours and forty-eight minutes (a record that would stand until 1952). In that time a sister ship, RMS *Queen Elizabeth*, was nearing completion on Clydebank. In several ways her design was an advance on that of *Queen Mary*. She had more efficient engines and with only two funnels had more space on the top deck, giving her a modern uncluttered look. She was also

Above: Cunard-White Star's *Queen Mary* was more traditional in appearance than the *Normandie* but proved immensely popular until her retirement in 1967. She survives to this day, moored in Long Beach, California as one of the Historic Hotels of America.

the world's biggest liner, 314 metres (1,031 ft) long and displacing 83,673 tons. She was also very well equipped, with 800 telephones and twenty-one lifts. It so happened that a second *Mauretania* had been launched in 1938, the first having been broken up in 1935. The new ship was built at Birkenhead by the Cammell Laird shipyard. Although smaller than *Queen Elizabeth*, with her twin funnels *Mauretania* had a similar modern appearance and the two would sometimes be confused at a distance.

The new *Queen Elizabeth* had still not been completely fitted out when war was declared in September 1939. Immediately, shipyard resources were diverted to naval ships, leaving the liner unfinished. Soon she was handed over to the amalgamated Cunard-White Star Line, painted all-over grey

and rigged with electromagnetic devices to prevent her hull from triggering magnetic mines. Intelligence had indicated she would be a prime target for the Luftwaffe, so instead of going to Southampton she made a dash under sealed orders to the safety of New York. There she joined *Queen Mary* and *Normandie* to form a trio of the three biggest liners in the world. Also present was the new *Mauretania*. For some months the four flagships awaited their fate to be gutted and fitted out as troopships.

◇◇◇◇◇◇◇◇◇◇◇◇◇◇◇◇◇◇◇◇◇◇◇◇

Thus ended the great era of transatlantic travel on liners that represented the apogee of comfort and elegance. Yet even after the end of the Second World War, ocean liners were still the chief means of mass intercontinental travel, and would remain so for the next decade or two. Thereafter, most potential passengers lacked the time to spend days on a journey, and increasingly opted to spend hours flying.

Opposite page bottom: The second *Mauretania* at Southampton's Western Dock in April 1949. After meritorious war service and refurbishment she had returned to the transatlantic run with added dollar-earning cruises in winter. But the market was changing. By 1960 she was running at a loss and was finally scrapped in 1965.

From left to right, *Normandie, Queen Mary* and *Queen Elizabeth* in New York in March 1940. All three liners were in the process of being converted to troopships.

2

PLANES

Of all mankind's technological achievements, the ability to fly has probably been the most momentous and with the furthest-reaching consequences, not least in matters of the imagination. From the earliest hominid there can scarcely have been a single individual who at some time hasn't enviously watched birds in their swiftness and elegance and wondered what such mastery of the air would feel like. It took us a long time to find out.

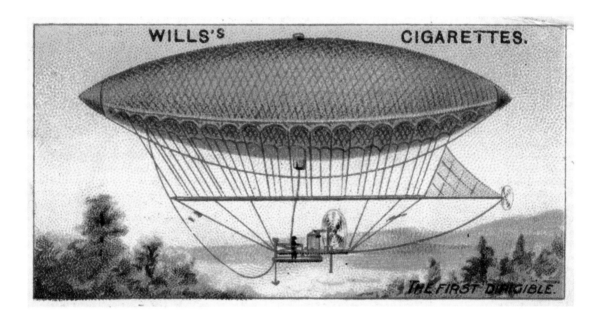

In 1784 the French mathematician and engineer Jean Baptiste Meusnier designed a hydrogen-filled dirigible with the elliptical shape of a rugby ball – hence to some degree 'streamlined' and showing an intention for it to move in a determined direction, possibly even against the wind. The ordinary hot air or hydrogen balloons of the period were round and simply drifted on the wind, like those of today. In the absence of an engine Meusnier planned to use oars for propulsion, so his design could never have worked as intended. His compatriot Henri Giffard's dirigible of 1852 looked quite similar although the envelope was slimmer, more pointed and more streamlined. This, however, was steam powered (a 3-horsepower engine driving a propeller) and was the world's first steerable (i.e. *dirigible*) passenger airship, making a first flight of almost 17 miles (27 km), including turns. This was a real

Henri Giffard's airship of 1852 was not only the first dirigible, it was aerodynamically designed for minimum wind resistance. Its main drawback was being steam-powered. Alas, it pre-dated the invention of petrol-driven engines by at least three decades.

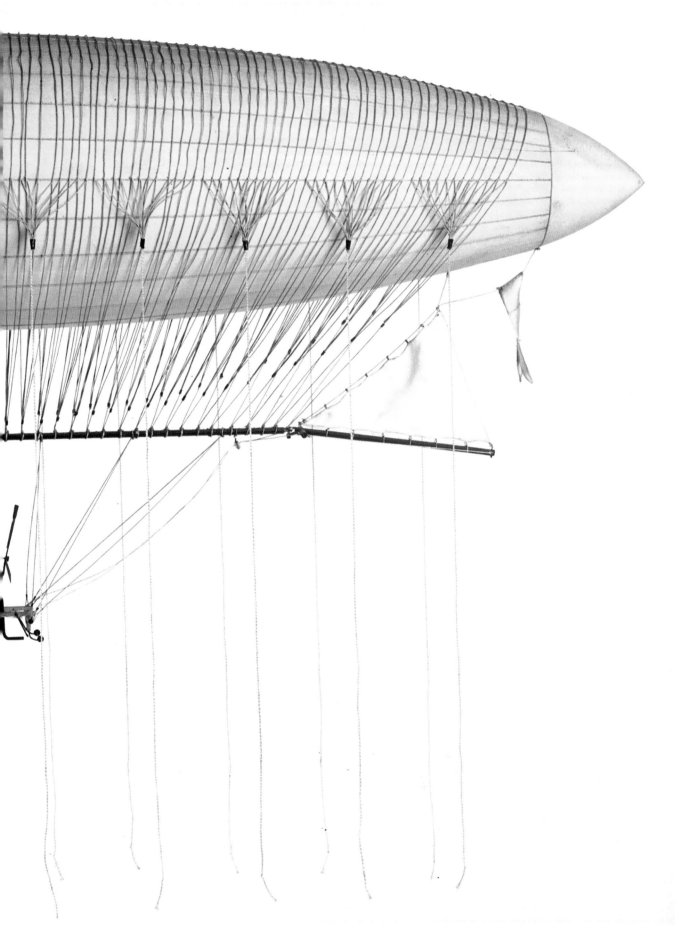

breakthrough even though steam engines were too heavy and offered the real danger of a fatal fire when used in conjunction with a hydrogen-filled envelope. So there the matter rested until the invention of a suitable internal combustion engine.

The man who single-handedly clung to the idea of the airship as a practical and economical mode of travel, able to circumnavigate the globe over land or sea, was Count Ferdinand von Zeppelin. He was a career military man in the German army until 1890 when, thanks to his unwise complaint to Kaiser Wilhelm II that the army of Württemberg was always being commanded by Prussian officers, he was summarily sacked from the rank of lieutenant-general. The trauma this caused blighted his life and he retired to his castle on the shores of Lake Constance to agonise about his future. Meanwhile, up in Pomerania at the other end of Germany, Otto Lilienthal was experimenting with hang gliders, and the possibility of powered flight was everywhere being discussed. Having read of these pioneering glider flights Ferdinand von Zeppelin decided where his new career lay. His dream was of large dirigibles that, instead of having to rely on steam for power, could now be fitted with internal combustion engines. Being filled with hydrogen gas they would have no need to generate lift by means of flimsy wings modelled on those of birds, like Lilienthal's. By sheer dint of scrimping and begging the count raised enough money to bring his hopes to fruition when in 1900 his first airship, LZ1, was eased out of its floating wooden hangar near Friedrichshafen to make a troubled short flight over Lake Constance, to the utter astonishment of onlookers.

Their amazement was mainly at the airship's sheer size, for it was a monster. At 128 metres (420 ft) long it was at the time by far the largest manmade object ever to fly. What made it truly revolutionary was its construction. All its balloon antecedents, including Giffard's, had been 'blimps': inflatables that relied for their shape on the pressure of gas inside a rubberised fabric outer skin. This first Zeppelin was radically different, being rigid. Its cigar shape was maintained by a vast and complex aluminium framework over which lay the taut outer skin. Inside the huge internal space were seventeen great gas cells that buoyed it aloft.

◇◇◇◇◇◇◇◇◇◇◇◇◇◇◇◇◇◇◇◇◇◇◇◇◇◇

From then on Zeppelin's progress was one of fits and starts as he formed a company and tried simultaneously to raise money for his invention's development and recruit a team of engineers with the requisite knowledge for this new and arcane mode of transport. In due course, the Wright

Opposite: Count Ferdinand von Zeppelin was an aviation pioneer on a par with the Wright brothers. By 1907, when winged aircraft could barely lift the weight of a single pilot, his enormous dirigibles could carry three tons of ballast plus eleven passengers for flights of several hours.

Otto Lilienthal makes one of his more than 2,000 hang-glider flights in northern Germany. By the time the last of these killed him in 1896 he was internationally celebrated for his work on wing design, above all by the Wright brothers.

brothers in 1903 and Blériot in 1909 demonstrated that powered flight of steerable heavier-than-air aircraft was possible over modest distances, but Zeppelin's dream was orders of magnitude more ambitious. He knew it would be many years before aircraft would be capable of carrying any sort of reasonable payload, whereas he was envisaging enormous dirigibles soon carrying many passengers and freight over almost limitless distances.

Before long he had attracted two men who were geniuses in their fields: Dr Ludwig Dürr, a brilliant design engineer, and Dr Hugo Eckener, who soon became a far-sighted director of Zeppelin's company and would also turn out to be an exceptionally gifted airship pilot. Under the aegis of such men the airships (which soon everyone called 'Zeppelins') improved by trial and error. There were crashes and setbacks, but the successes quickly attracted widespread public attention. Soon the huge airships were viewed in Germany as a source of national pride and enough cash resulted from appeals to keep the company going. By the summer of 1914, and to the count's disgust, it was obvious that his Zeppelins would be requisitioned for military use in the war. After all, they were by far the world's largest aircraft and with the greatest lifting power. By contrast most early winged aircraft of the day could barely lift more than a single pilot, whereas a Zeppelin with its multiple powerful Maybach engines could carry a crew of several men and a considerable cargo on flights lasting many hours and covering hundreds of miles.

Hence it was Zeppelins that carried out the first German bombing raids over England. For a considerable time they bombed cities like London by night and without effective opposition. They did have their weaknesses, however. Some were pinpointed by searchlights and shot down by anti-aircraft guns; eventually others would be sent down in flames by aircraft whose technology was improving rapidly under the pressure of war; still others went out of control and soared to altitudes where their crews became unconscious from oxygen starvation or froze to death. Several simply disappeared for ever over the North Sea. By 1917 their only defence against night fighters firing incendiary bullets into their vulnerable hydrogen gas bags lay in sheer altitude. New, much lighter Zeppelins were designed that could fly at 20,000 feet where they would be safer, since at that time few Allied fighters of the period could surpass an altitude of 13,000 feet or so. The old count would never see for himself how his company's new airships could outfly the latest enemy fighters, for Ferdinand von Zeppelin died in early 1917. His name had long become synonymous with that of a revolutionary form of aerial transport. By now the company, bolstered by government funding, was very much a going concern building innovative new airships at its factory at Friedrichshafen on Lake Constance.

On 21 November that same year, Zeppelin L59 was ordered to undertake an astonishing journey that would have confirmed all Count Ferdinand's expectations for his remarkable invention. Carrying a crew of twenty-two the airship took off from Yambol in Bulgaria, heavily laden with 15 tons of medical supplies as well as with further tons of guns and ammunition. These were desperately needed by General Paul von Lettow-Vorbeck, who was fighting a guerrilla campaign against British forces in German East Africa. After months of brilliant bush tactics the general was beleaguered by numerically superior forces in the Makonde highlands of what today is southeast Tanzania. The L59 left Bulgaria, flew south across Turkey and Crete, crossed Egypt and continued down through Sudan to a point 125 miles (201 km) west of Khartoum. Here it received a coded radio message from Berlin saying that General von Lettow-Vorbeck had surrendered and the airship should return home at once. In actual fact the news was untrue and the general was fighting on, but the L59's commander had no way of knowing this and there was no alternative but to turn around in the air. The Zeppelin flew all the way back to Bulgaria where it landed on 25 November. It had been an astonishing feat: a nonstop flight of 4,200 miles (6,759 km) in ninety-five hours. It was the first true intercontinental flight and had been achieved without landing or refuelling. No other nation on earth could match this technology.

In the aftermath of Germany's defeat in 1918, Hugo Eckener and Ludwig Dürr considered themselves lucky. The war might be lost but both they and their families had been spared, and so had the Zeppelin factory and airship sheds in Ludwigshafen. On balance their airships had not been a great success as bombers, but both men remained convinced of their future as long-distance peacetime passenger-carriers. The route they had in mind was the lucrative transatlantic one, for airships could travel three times as fast as even the quickest liner. The men's determination now was to show how Zeppelins could rival and even better the speed and luxury of pre-war first-class travel while offering passengers stunning aerial panoramas.

At this point the punitive terms of the Versailles Treaty struck, in the form of the Inter-Allied Control Commission. Unsurprisingly, this forbade the Zeppelin company to build any military airships. However, it also restricted commercial ones to a gas capacity that was too small for Eckener and Dürr's planned transatlantic service. Then in June 1919 came the first nonstop Atlantic crossing by an aircraft: Alcock and Brown's flight in a converted Vickers Vimy bomber at an average speed of 118 mph (190 kph). This was

The LZ1 Zeppelin's first flight in 1900 was not in itself a great success and lasted a mere eighteen minutes. However, it did give its astounded witnesses the chance to see the biggest and heaviest manmade object ever to become airborne.

daring and impressive; but it was still obvious that it would be many years yet before fixed-wing aircraft could safely achieve such a journey with a payload of passengers. Then only weeks later the British airship R34, itself modelled on Zeppelin's L33, made the first Atlantic crossing from east to west, the notoriously harder way even for ships since it was against the prevailing wind. The Zeppelin company's much depleted staff must have ground their teeth with frustration.

Then in 1922 came an unexpected reprieve when the US navy ordered an airship from the company. The specification was for twenty passengers with sleeping accommodation – a first for any aircraft. It was also to have a radio room, washrooms and a lavatory, as well as an all-electric kitchen. (No naked flames were ever permitted on hydrogen-filled airships. Before boarding, passengers were always frisked for any lighters, matches and cigarettes they might absent-mindedly have overlooked.) The beautiful silver Zeppelin LZ126 was duly delivered to the United States in 1924, flown across the Atlantic by Hugo Eckener himself. It generated patriotic enthusiasm in Germany and a tumult of car horns welcomed it as it arrived over the Statue of Liberty.

This first transatlantic flight by a genuine Zeppelin marked the turning point in the company's fortunes. With the business contacts Eckener now established in the US (such as with the Goodyear Company) enthusiasm for the possibilities offered by airship travel grew steadily and did much to reverse the resentment that had been caused by the Zeppelins' involvement in the war. The German airships had, after all, been commandeered rather than volunteered. Then in 1925 the Treaty of Locarno rescinded the limits on the size of commercial airships. In theory this meant the Zeppelin Company could go ahead with Eckener's dream of a truly huge airship. In practice the company could not afford it, being limited by the size of the factory and hangar on Lake Constance. Yet it could still build a big enough airship to demonstrate the possibilities of a regular transatlantic service with fare-paying passengers, bags of mail and other freight. Eckener's vision was agreeably romantic, even evangelical. In his own words he wanted 'an airship in which one would not merely fly but also be able to *voyage*, a Zeppelin that was also a training ship with a pioneering mission, not only for airships but for all kinds of flight above the oceans.'[1]

The Zeppelin bombing raids on Britain in the First World War seemed to bear out H. G. Wells's prediction of terror from the skies and caused much panic. Yet the giant craft soon became vulnerable to improvements in anti-aircraft gunnery and fighter aircraft.

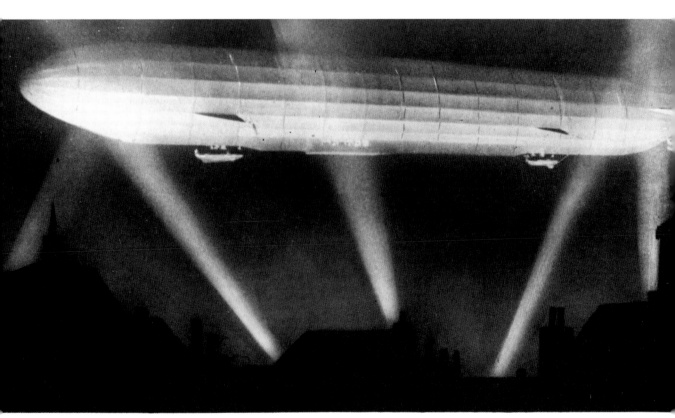

Previous spread: The British airship R34 was largely a copy of Zeppelin's L33. In 1919, a bare fortnight after Alcock and Brown's west-to-east first transatlantic flight, R34 made the first (and harder) east-to-west crossing. Regular transatlantic flights became at least imaginable.

The new venture was, as usual, designed by Dr Dürr and intended to represent the very best of Zeppelin technology. In 1928, on the anniversary of the old count's death, his daughter named the magnificent new airship *Graf Zeppelin* in his honour. This was LZ127, which everyone soon knew simply as 'the *Graf*'. It at once made several long-distance journeys throughout Germany and quickly established that in handling and in every other respect it was a great advance on all its predecessors. In October it finally lifted off for its first transatlantic journey despite meteorological reports of severe bad weather along its projected route.

In addition to the forty crew, 66,000 items of air mail and a pet canary, there were twenty passengers – among them Count Zeppelin's son-in-law Count Brandenstein-Zeppelin, the Prussian Minister of the Interior, four representatives of the German Air Ministry, two foreign airship experts, six representatives of German and international newspapers, two artists to depict whatever the photographers could not, and an insurance expert to assess the risks of commercial airship flights.[2]

Thanks to appalling weather over the Atlantic the flight was very nearly a disaster and the *Graf* came perilously close to ditching in the ocean – which at that time, many decades before GPS, would almost certainly have proved fatal to all on board. Yet with outstanding piloting, an airship that proved to be remarkably tough structurally, passengers who did not panic and a good deal of luck, the *Graf Zeppelin* finally landed in the United States despite damage to its tail. The flight, with its enormous detours to avoid the worst of the

The *Graf Zeppelin's* passengers have lunch in the airship's saloon during its round-the-world trip. The chef, Otto Manz, beams from the left of the picture. The modernist pillars and ceiling panels consort oddly with the chintziness of the curtains.

weather, had taken 111 hours and forty-four minutes for a journey of 6,168 miles (9,926 km), easily beating the L59's wartime flight to Africa and back in 1917. The American public had already heard radio broadcasts suggesting the airship was lost. When news reached New York that it had survived and was nearing the city, the turnout of cheering crowds in the streets, together with the blaring of motor horns, resulted in a tumult that reached the *Graf*'s passengers a few hundred feet overhead who later claimed the noise had practically drowned out the roar of the airship's engines.

What the trip had shown was that while the *Graf* was extremely resilient and could survive much, it was not yet a completely all-weather design. The journey back was equally beset by storms, but they made it home to Ludwigshafen in just short of seventy-two hours. From the point of view of arousing commercial interest, the trip had ignited Zeppelin fever across the United States. In terms of public relations it proved even more valuable, having done much to bring about a rapprochement a decade after the end of the First World War. The Zeppelin Company were in no doubt that with a bit more development, airships represented the future of air travel – in particular, for passengers who wanted the novel experience of panoramic aerial views of the planet from big observation windows, on voyages that could offer stately luxury as well as adventure.

◇◇◇◇◇◇◇◇◇◇◇◇◇◇◇◇◇◇◇◇◇◇

By now it was 1929. While airship technology had been improving, so had that of conventional aviation and it was a fertile period for setting world records of all kinds. On 7 January that year an American aircraft stayed aloft for six days with primitive but effective air-to-air refuelling, thereby breaking the *Graf Zeppelin*'s recent duration record. By mid-year even this six-day flight would be beaten several times, the last occasion being between 13 and 30 July when two pilots stayed in the air above St Louis, Missouri for seventeen days, twelve hours and seventeen minutes in a Curtiss Robin. Apart from the fortitude of the pilots, this feat spoke volumes for the increased reliability of aero engines.

As regards distance, 1929 saw a nonstop unrefuelled flight by two Spaniards from Seville to Bahia in Brazil. They achieved this in one of the greatest of post-war French aircraft, a Breguet 19 biplane, and covered a distance of 4,275 miles (6,880 km). In altitude, too, a new world record was set in May 1929 by the German pilot Willi Neunhofer. Flying an all-metal Junkers W34 monoplane he reached a height of 42,123 feet.

Above: Henry Segrave's *Golden Arrow* at Daytona Beach in March 1929 setting a new world record of 231.45 mph (372.48 kph). The car's 23.9-litre Napier Lion engine also powered over 160 different aircraft types in the 1920s.

Right: F/O H. R. D. Waghorn taxies out at Calshot in 1929 in his Supermarine S6A to win the Schneider Trophy with a speed of 328.63 mph (528.88 kph). As can be seen, his forward vision was virtually nil. This aircraft was later destroyed in a fatal accident.

But what really caught the public's imagination were absolute speed records, and particularly the way in which aircraft had effortlessly overtaken cars. In March 1929 the British driver Henry Segrave set a new land speed record of 231 mph (372 kph); but back in 1924 a French aircraft had already established a world record air speed of 278.37 mph (447.99 kph). Now in September 1929 a British Supermarine S6 floatplane achieved 357.7 mph (575.7 kph). That it was a floatplane was significant because it was designed for a Schneider Trophy race. Inaugurated in 1913 by the French aviation enthusiast Jacques Schneider, these annual races over water would turn out to be the most important spur – other than war – to improved designs for both airframes and aero engines. On the face of it, it was extraordinary that such an aircraft should set a world air speed record since its floats were an obvious source of considerable drag, no matter how streamlined the fuselage and wings. Over the years the fuselages of these competing aircraft were indeed progressively streamlined to the eventual point where the pilot had practically no direct forward vision and had to squint through side windows past the shrouded engine exhausts. It is hardly surprising that they were difficult and dangerous machines to fly, and there were sundry fatalities. Nonetheless, they led to the progressive streamlining of aero engines, with the in-line banks of cylinders in a flattened vee typical of the Rolls-Royce Merlin that would soon become one of the most significant engines of the Second World War.

Such highly specialised competition aircraft might have been in a class of their own, but the knowledge they yielded was swiftly incorporated into more domestic designs. Still in 1929, and as a final reminder to the Zeppelin Company that the commercial aviation world was not standing still, the American Air Transport Association published figures showing that scheduled airlines in the US were already flying forty-two flights daily and had a network of 102 cities linked by over 33,000 route miles. True, these were not luxurious flights. Aircraft such as the Ford Trimotor (aka the 'Tin Goose') could carry eleven passengers at a modest cruising speed of 95 mph (153 kph) for a maximum of 475 miles (764 km) – less if against a headwind. Yet despite that year's stock market crash, increasing numbers of Americans found air travel vastly preferable to covering long distances in unreliable automobiles along rural roads. Besides, thanks to celebrated record-breakers of both sexes, flying had acquired real glamour. It was *modern*. It smacked of Progress and better things to come.

Also in 1929, Britain's Imperial Airways inaugurated its flights to India. Three years earlier the company had begun flying a regular service to

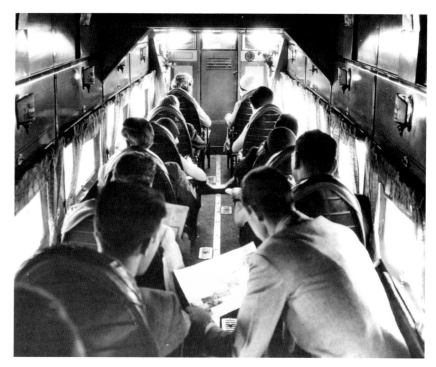

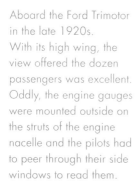

Aboard the Ford Trimotor
in the late 1920s.
With its high wing, the
view offered the dozen
passengers was excellent.
Oddly, the engine gauges
were mounted outside on
the struts of the engine
nacelle and the pilots had
to peer through their side
windows to read them.

Baghdad via Cairo in de Havilland Hercules aircraft: three-engined biplanes that could carry mail and seven passengers on a series of long drawn-out hops in no great comfort. The new Indian service was a little more glamorous, there being only one class of ticket: first. Not all the initial stages of the journey were even flown. The twenty passengers first embarked in a large three-engined Armstrong Whitworth Argosy biplane in Croydon, whence they flew to Geneva. There they disembarked and travelled overnight by train in Pullman sleepers to Genoa. The next morning they went out in launches to board a Short Calcutta flying boat moored in the harbour. This, too, was a big three-engined biplane that was also the world's first metal-hulled seaplane. In it they flew down to Rome where they were given a day's rest to prepare for the somewhat gruelling onward journey. Thereafter they flew slowly in stages to Karachi over several days (the Calcutta cruised at a dignified 97 mph [156 kph] and had a range of around 600 miles [966 km]). However, each night they would sleep at the best hotels that cities like Cairo could offer. On reaching Karachi they transferred back to an Argosy for the final flight down to Bombay, where they must have disembarked with their heads ringing with engine noise and lurching from the constant motion like sailors ashore. Flying to India in 1929 was indeed slow; but it was still far quicker than doing the journey by sea, which in some quarters was beginning to seem a rather old-fashioned way of getting about the globe.

The de Havilland DH 66 Hercules was designed for Imperial Airways' Cairo-to-Baghdad route. Having three engines was considered a safeguard against a possible forced landing in the desert. G-EBMW was the prototype and first flew in 1926.

PLAYER'S CIGARETTES

G-AACH

ARMSTRONG WHITWORTH "ARGOSY"

Armstrong Whitworth's AW 154 Argosy also dated from 1926 and was the first aircraft anywhere to fly a 'named' air service: the luxury 'Silver Wing' flights between London and Paris, for which two seats were replaced by a bar manned by a white-coated steward.

The following year Imperial Airways began flights to South Africa, using four-engined Handley Page HP42/45 aircraft. These were still big biplanes, although now most of the fuselage was metal even if the wings and tail surfaces were fabric-covered. What this new service unquestionably offered was stateliness. Flights from Croydon to Cape Town might take anywhere between four and seven days, depending on headwinds and storms. The aircraft could manage only 90 mph (145 kph) but so far as was possible the twenty-six passengers were cosseted. Again, these were first-class-only flights. The aircraft was divided into three sections, all of which offered great physical comfort with plenty of legroom. There was the saloon, where hot meals were properly served on chinaware with silver cutlery; a smoking section; and a bar and cocktails area. All drinks were free. Each day in late

Introduced in 1928, and the mainstay of the Mediterranean-to-Karachi leg of Imperial Airways' flights to India, the Short S8 Calcutta was the world's first metal-hulled flying boat. Flights at a maximum 97 mph (156 kph) would have seemed endless to its fifteen passengers.

afternoon the aircraft would put down and the passengers would spend the night in the best hotels on offer in Rome or Naples, Cairo, Khartoum and Victoria Falls.

Yet it is easy to stress the plusher aspects of this first-class travel by overlooking the major problem of air-sickness. These aircraft on the empire routes were deliberately designed to be able to land and take off from grass, which necessitated comparatively low landing and take-off speeds. This in turn meant a big wing area for the weight. The upshot was that they were very susceptible to atmospheric disturbances, air pockets and lurches and bumps. They wallowed their way grandly, but anyone susceptible to motion sickness could suffer abominably. On the plus side, by 1939 Imperial Airways' HP42/45 airliners, mocked by Anthony Fokker for being so slow, had chalked up ten years' service without a single accident casualty – a record that was almost certainly unique in those interwar years of commercial flying when fearful crashes or complete disappearances were commonplace.

At that time passengers on long-distance flights had a third alternative to airships and airliners in the shape of the flying boat. The 1930s was par excellence the era of the great flying boats that in both theory and advertisement boasted the romance, comfort and amenities of liner travel while being many times faster. By today's standards, long journeys in flying boats could prove less than magical owing to the intrusive engine noise. Apart from that they were not designed to fly high, so the cabin was unpressurised and could become so achingly cold it was not unknown for the water in a passenger's glass to freeze. Because they could seldom climb above bad weather they would often get the worst of bumpy conditions. In fact, flying boat journeys of the day frequently offered sensitive passengers

Opposite: The Handley Page HP42/45 was a genuine attempt at first-class air travel. The cutaways of the aircraft give some idea of their luxurious cabin arrangements.

IMPERIAL AIRWAYS
THE GREATEST AIR SERVICE IN THE WORLD

The all-metal, three-engined Junkers G24 of 1925 heralded a new era in aircraft design and became the workhorse of Germany's new national airline. It inaugurated the world's first passenger night flights and was furnished with instruments for blind flying.

the romantic opportunity to be both airsick and seasick, since if the sea was choppy on landing it could make for a difficult transhipment from aircraft to launch and from launch to jetty.

In connection with these long-distance routes it should be remembered that Britain had the advantage of a huge empire. A global network of coaling stops had long been established for her merchant shipping fleet, most particularly on routes to the Middle and Far East. A flying boat on either the India or South Africa route was never further than a few hundred miles from a small port where it could put down and guarantee to find fuel, mechanical assistance, a telegraph office and English spoken. Despite this, one of the obvious disadvantages of the earlier flying boats was that, except for short overland hops or unless there was a convenient large river or series of lakes along the way, they were often obliged to remain in sight of coastlines, which was seldom the quickest or most economical route to their destination.

⬦⬦⬦⬦⬦⬦⬦⬦⬦⬦⬦⬦⬦⬦⬦⬦⬦⬦⬦⬦⬦

A.-B. Aerotransports tremotors sjöflygplan "Uppland" Linien Stockholm-Helsingfors.

Back in Germany, meanwhile, civil aviation was also flourishing in the Zeppelins' home territory. In 1926 the Junkers aircraft company had produced its advanced trimotor G24 passenger aircraft. This was an all-metal monoplane skinned with aluminium alloy that was corrugated for strength: a highly successful feature that Junkers had pioneered in the war. The G24 was too obviously the model for the Ford Trimotor – so much so that Junkers twice sued Ford for patent infringement and won both times. The G24 carried two crew and fourteen passengers and could cruise at 106 mph (171 kph) with a range of 410 miles (660 km). The year 1926 also saw the German airline Deutsche Luft Hansa founded, inaugurating flights from Berlin to Moscow as well as to Zürich, Königsberg (today's Kaliningrad) and several other widely separated German cities. In its first year of operations the airline flew 56,268 passengers and 560 tons of mail and freight nearly 3.75 million flight miles.

However, it is easy to be misled by the far larger number of passengers than that of the tonnage of mail and freight. The fact is that not for another decade would any airline make much profit out of carrying passengers. The first fledgling airlines were mostly started more as postal services, especially where lines of communication were thousands of miles long, as in the United States and the British and French empires. Aeromarine West Indies Airways was a short-lived Florida airline that in 1921 began carrying mail and passengers from Key West to Havana and the Bahamas. It went out of business in 1924, not because the supply of passengers dried up but because the US Post Office cancelled its contract. As its chief executive, Inglis M. Uppercu, had gloomily remarked in 1923: 'You cannot get one nickel for commercial flying.' It would be many years before the president of American Airlines, C. R. Smith, could remark fondly of the Douglas DC-3, 'It was the first airplane… that could make money just by hauling passengers.'

◇◇◇◇◇◇◇◇◇◇◇◇◇◇◇◇◇◇◇◇◇◇◇◇◇◇◇◇

By 1929, therefore, the Zeppelin Airship Company knew it was not short of competition in the rapidly growing market for carrying mail and freight that alone could cover the cost of passengers. The Zeppelins' ace was that they could carry much more freight than any conventional aircraft. But then a challenger appeared, and alarmingly close to home. In order to avoid the restrictions on Germany-based aircraft manufacturers imposed by the post-war controls, the German aircraft company Dornier had moved just over the border into Switzerland. They were now close neighbours of the Zeppelin works, their new factory and immense sheds being little more

than a few kilometres away across Lake Constance. On 12 July 1929 they were readying the world's largest seaplane, the twelve-engined Dornier Do-X, for its maiden flight. Zeppelin company workers could well have had a grandstand view of this extraordinary event. The Do-X was enormous. With the sole exception of a Russian monster which the Dornier outweighed, it was easily the world's largest winged aircraft. It was a twelve-engined monoplane, and with ten to fourteen crew it was designed to carry 100 passengers on short hauls and sixty-six on longer distances. It had three decks and was furnished to rival the standards set by the great transatlantic liners with sleeping berths, lavatories, a bar, a smoking room, a dining room and an all-electric galley. The Zeppelin company could hardly have failed to see the challenge to their prized *Graf* that this astonishing new seaplane posed, as its twelve engines howled and it took off from the lake in a huge flurry of spray. After testing, the Do-X left on a leisurely journey lasting several months, flying down the west coast of Africa and across to Brazil, thereafter making her way up to New York at a stately pace interrupted by mechanical repairs. Three examples were built and duly became very popular with passengers. But the Do-X was an unwieldy monster and was soon overtaken by technological advances that made for nimbler designs. All three Dorniers would be scrapped in 1937, but not before they must have occasioned the Zeppelin company some rueful and even panicky reflections back in 1929.

As a result, that spring, Zeppelin decided to raise the *Graf*'s public visibility by organising an 'Orient Flight' to Egypt and inviting twenty-seven carefully selected VIPs for the trip: politicians, important civil servants, the president of the Reichstag, leading journalists and celebrities. The *Graf* took off on the first day of spring in Dr Eckener's safe hands. The weather was still cold and at first the passengers froze, although there were 63 quarts of wine aboard and 160 bottles of spirits to give an illusion of warmth. (This generous budgeting allowed the passengers six bottles of spirits apiece for a journey of less than four days, so there must have been some spectacular topers aboard.) Certain of the English-speaking journalists might have read a book of Lowell Thomas's that had been published the previous year. Thomas was the American journalist and traveller who had first given global publicity to Lawrence of Arabia, and in *European Skyways* he had sagely remarked, '…if you happen to do any flying in early spring or late autumn, or during the winter, you will have far more peace of mind if you wear heavyweight woollen stockings.' His was the voice of experience. However, despite the initial cold the trip afforded

Opposite top: Dornier's mammoth 12-engined Do-X flying boat of 1929. With its three decks and dining room it was expressly designed to rival the transatlantic liners in terms of passenger comfort. Unfortunately it overstepped the mark and was a commercial failure.

Opposite bottom: As can be seen, with its basketwork seats and stark metal bracing the interior of the Dornier Do-X did not much suggest luxury travel. It was a brave attempt to outdo the airship as a swift alternative to sea travel for up to 100 passengers.

the *Graf*'s complement some sensational air tourism as the great airship crossed the French Riviera and then overflew Rome before drifting low over Capri and finally Vesuvius at sunset. In the morning the passengers ate breakfast over Crete, thereafter lunched above Cyprus and at sunset hovered with stilled engines above Jerusalem with the Dome of the Rock directly below. When the Dead Sea came into view the irrepressible Dr Eckener took a decision:

> *I now had the idea of offering the guests a sensation of a quite extraordinary kind. The surface of the Dead Sea lies almost 1,300 feet below sea level. We were irresistibly tempted by the opportunity to fly our Zeppelin at an altitude well below sea level. The barely risen full moon shone still with little power, so that the great lake lay reflected in semi-darkness, as mysterious as the nether world. We slowly sank down, carefully feeling our way lower and lower, until we hovered a few hundred feet over the surface of the water. We looked up to the heights towering around us as if from a cellar. It was a strange sensation to be in a ship which ordinarily soars high above sea level, now flying some thousand feet below it. We opened a couple of bottles of Rhine wine and celebrated the occasion, which each of us found unique.*[3]

The *Graf Zeppelin* approaching Rio de Janeiro in May 1930. In the year following his epic round-the-world voyage, Dr Eckener was keen to visit other parts of the globe to sound out the possibilities for a regular airship service.

It is an odd thought that in 1929 the deepest descent most military submarines could safely manage was little more than 300 feet, meaning that the *Graf* and its passengers were roughly four times further below sea level than anyone had ever been. Only in the next few years would the great American pioneers William Beebe and Otis Barton exceed such depths in the Bathysphere, which was a cramped and freezing steel ball lowered at the end of a cable. By contrast, dinner aboard the *Graf* that evening as it rose once more into the desert air was leisured and celebratory.

The 'Orient Flight' was a great success despite the cold. In three and a half days the passengers had covered 5,000 miles (over 8,000 km) – equivalent to an average speed of 61 mph (98 kph) – and had seen some

A stereograph of the *Graf Zeppelin* over the Great Pyramid on its 'Orient Flight' in the spring of 1929. This was a short luxury trip designed to attract support for the airship's more ambitious circumnavigation later that year.

of the most famous destinations on the tourist map at a leisurely pace from a few hundred feet overhead. It was enough to convince Dr Eckener that he should attempt the grandest of all journeys: a flight around the world. By 1929 several aircraft had managed this circumnavigation, but only in many stages on journeys that lasted weeks and without carrying a single passenger. Furthermore, the routes these pioneers took had to be carefully planned to include places where the aircraft could refuel. In particular, this made island-hopping across the vast expanse of the Pacific a nail-biting affair of navigation – in those days a matter of dead reckoning, aided by a compass and even sextant sightings taken from the cockpit. And of course there was always the risk of unexpected headwinds and tropical storms that could blow up out of nowhere.

Dr Eckener decided that the best way of convincing sceptics of the airship's true versatility as the transport of the future was to choose a route that would be virtually impossible for any aircraft of the day, and to do it with a complement of passengers, stores and freight in the full glare of international publicity. Only thus, and by risking encounter with the widest variety of weather conditions, could the true strength of Zeppelin travel be demonstrated. Accordingly, he planned for the *Graf* to fly a 7,000-mile north-eastward route across the endless taiga and tundra of Siberia to the Kamchatka Peninsula, then down the Sea of Okhotsk to Japan, to make the first landing in Tokyo. After that, across the Pacific to the United States and so on back to Europe.

This was unquestionably risky; but if all went according to plan it would afford the passengers the trip of a lifetime at no great discomfort. Yet even this ambitious gamble needs to be put into historical context. That long haul through Central Asia – largely unmapped and untravelled by any Westerner – had already been crossed overland by machine. This was in the Peking to Paris 'race' for cars back in 1907 at a time when it could never have been done by air (Blériot had yet to cross the Channel). The race had been far less a test of speed than of mechanical ruggedness on the part of the cars and their drivers' physical stamina. It took place as the result of a gauntlet flung down in the Paris newspaper *Le Matin* on 31 January 1907. 'What needs to be proved today,' the challenger wrote, 'is that as long as a man has a car, he can do anything and go anywhere. Is there anyone who will undertake to travel this summer from Peking to Paris by automobile?' In its way, this made Dr Eckener's proposed round-the-world trip look almost easy since for most of the way across Asia there were no roads and no maps. Caches of petrol for the cars had to be left in advance by camel train. The drivers did their best to follow a lone telegraph line as it wandered westwards across ravines and rivers, over trackless Mongolia (where one car broke down in the desert and by sheer luck the driver was found by some locals half dead from thirst), and through equally trackless Siberia. Incredibly, the winner managed the 9,317 miles (14,994 km) from the French Embassy in Peking to Paris in sixty-one days. He was the Italian Prince Borghese driving an immense Itala that at various times had been pushed by teams of coolies, pulled by oxen and rescued from a wooden bridge that collapsed beneath its weight. The trip had been well followed by newspapers because each car's co-driver was a journalist who stopped periodically to tap out a message wherever the telegraph came to earth in a village hut.

The *Graf Zeppelin*'s circumnavigation was to be even better covered by the press. Since the American Hearst newspaper empire was paying for much of the trip in exchange for exclusive coverage rights, the momentous voyage had to begin with the *Graf* first flying from Friedrichshafen to Lakehurst Naval Air Station, New Jersey. It was at William Randolph Hearst's own insistence that the circumnavigation should start and end there. Having done that, the *Graf* then flew back to Friedrichshafen for five days while the engines were checked, and then on 15 August it finally lifted off for the long haul to Japan over parts of the globe that had yet to be mapped, let alone flown over. In addition to forty crew members there were twenty passengers aboard, some of whom had paid $7,000 (the equivalent today of $103,000 or £77,800), and others $9,000 ($133,000 or £100,000) for the privilege of enjoying this first-in-history, once-in-a-lifetime trip. All the passenger areas were in the great teardrop-shaped gondola that formed a graceful wart on the airship's chin. They chiefly consisted of a corridor with a row of sleeping cabins off each side, plus a washroom and lavatory at the end, and a large lounge or day room lined with observation windows that at meal times doubled as a dining saloon. This accommodation was not a patch on what a cruise liner could have offered its first-class passengers in terms of elegance and luxury; but the lucky few in the *Graf* thought of themselves as hand-picked pioneers and adventurers rather than drones. They were quite prepared to put up with cold and other hardships (such as not being able to smoke) in exchange for the journey of a lifetime watched by the world's press.

Once out of western Europe and heading over the Soviet Union the airship must have aroused incredulity and even superstitious fear on the ground the further eastwards it flew – because no one would ever have seen anything like it. The *Graf* was 245 metres (804 ft) long and 41 metres (135 ft) in diameter. It was propelled by five Maybach VL-2 engines, each of over

33 litres' capacity and together capable of driving the enormous craft along at 87 mph (140 kph). Virtually none of the few people living in the occasional primitive Russian village the *Graf* passed over would ever have heard the sound of engines coming from the sky, and the sight of this vast airborne thing must have struck terror into them; the passengers later gave accounts of watching people below scattering for cover. Yet the wretches on the ground were not the only ones to feel apprehension. The crew as well as passengers were fully aware that the further north and eastwards the Zeppelin flew, the further the chances lessened that they would ever be found if anything went wrong and the *Graf* needed to put down. Hours went by and hundreds of miles unrolled beneath the airship while the watchers in it could see no trace of human existence in the endless forests and bogs they were traversing. It was a safe bet that much of what they were observing had never before been seen by human eye.

And yet nothing did go wrong. There were nerve-wracking moments towards the end as the *Graf* flew over the uncharted Stanovoi mountains in low cloud, but finally they came safely out over the Sea of Okhotsk. It had taken them just over three days to reach the Far East from Friedrichshafen. Some hours later they alighted in Tokyo to a tumultuous welcome. At slightly under four days it was the furthest nonstop distance ever flown: 7,000 miles (11,265 km) in just under 102 hours. It was a distance (Dr Eckener noted triumphantly) that would have taken a month by fast liner and over a fortnight on the Trans-Siberian Railway. Thanks to Hearst newspapers the arrival in Japan was given front-page press coverage worldwide. After three days' exhausting receptions and replenishing of food stocks and fuel, Dr Eckener was thankful to lift the *Graf* back into the air on 22 August for the long onward flight to Los Angeles and New York. They soon ran into a vicious typhoon that threw them around before the airship emerged much shaken but unscathed – just the sort of extreme weather conditions needed to prove that it could survive.

On 25 August they reached San Francisco after a further 5,380 miles (8,658 km) of the Pacific crossing – the longest flight yet made over water. They put down near Los Angeles into the now-customary hordes of cameramen and crowds of cheering sightseers. Various impressed military men asserted that travel by dirigible could eventually render ocean travel obsolete. However, the onward flight to New York began with near-disaster. A severe atmospheric inversion typical of the Los Angeles area made the temperature on the ground much cooler than that above the layer, with the result that the *Graf* rose but sluggishly and only after a large weight of stores was jettisoned in order to gain it enough height to clear some high-tension power lines. A fatal accident was barely avoided by the skilful Dr Eckener; but the narrow squeak must have dimmed some of the new optimism about airships representing the future of long-distance transport. Thereafter all went well until finally they reached New York and triumphantly overflew the Statue of Liberty, which for Hearst marked the end of the flight he had partly sponsored. Their total flying time had been twelve days and eleven minutes, and including the stops the trip had lasted three weeks. Both were new world records. From then on it was an easy trip home to Friedrichshafen.

◇◇◇◇◇◇◇◇◇◇◇◇◇◇◇◇◇◇◇◇◇◇◇◇

One of the men on the world trip was Lieutenant-Commander Joachim Breithaupt. An old friend of Dr Eckener's, he had commanded a Zeppelin during the war until he was shot down and made a prisoner of war. He was aboard the *Graf* as the German Air Ministry's representative. In his final report he judged that rigid airships had a good commercial future flying passengers and high-value freight like mail, valuables and commercial samples where speed was essential. He said there was already considerable interest in a regular South America service; and where difficult terrain such as mountains, swampland and deserts made travel by rail or car difficult or impossible, the airship came into its own. 'However,' he ended, 'the public must be convinced that the airship is a safe, regular and comparably punctual mode of transport.'[4]

But then in October 1930 the badly built, overweight and underpowered British airship R101 crashed into a low hill in northern France on its maiden flight to India, exploding in a fireball that killed all but six of the fifty-four people aboard. It had been laden with crates of champagne, silverware for banquets in India, barrels of beer, a 600-foot-long blue carpet and a ton of personal luggage belonging to the air minister, Lord Thomson. At a single stroke the appalling loss of life gave new credence to those sceptical of airships who had been largely silenced by the *Graf Zeppelin*'s various triumphs. Hard-headed assessments were now increasingly heard that airships were inherently unsafe and, in the case of the R101, inequitable because it had been built at taxpayers' expense when with its Pullman-style luxury it was way beyond the means of ordinary people to travel on it. But the really telling criticism was that airships were essentially uncommercial. The first man to fly solo across the Atlantic, Charles Lindbergh, had once visited the *Graf* and was impressed by the comfortable cabins and well-appointed dining saloon. 'But only forty passengers for such an enormous aircraft?' he wondered. 'I can see no future for the airship. It is too slow, it has only half the speed of an airplane. Between the steamer and the airplane there is no niche for the rigid airship.'[5]

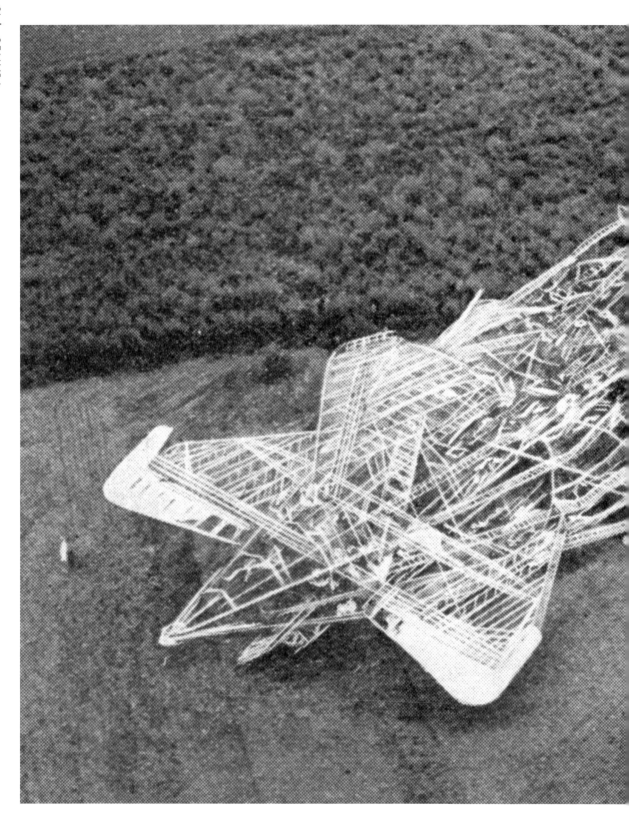

Previous spread: The skeletal remains in northern France of Britain's R101 in October 1930. Known as the 'socialist' ship for having been built at state expense, it was overburdened with complex technology. Its fiery end cast a pall over the future of airship travel.

In such remarks about the undemocratic and uncommercial nature of airship travel there was an uncanny foretaste of the criticisms that fifty years later would be aimed at Concorde. The world's first supersonic airliner brought glory to France and Britain much as the *Graf Zeppelin* had to Germany, and similar avowals were made about the unstoppable pace of the technological progress it represented. Even apart from the prodigious costs of its development and construction, ultimately funded by the taxpayers of France and Britain, Concorde could never conceivably have made any airline a profit. The aircraft's usual payload of executives, rock stars and their baggage formed a mere 6 per cent of its all-up weight, the largest proportion of the rest being fuel. Both the *Graf* and Concorde showed it is a simplistic error always to equate progress with anything that makes life more convenient or flashier for businesspeople and celebrities. Another popular mistake made about airships and Concorde alike was to assume – as many people still do – that air travel must inevitably involve ever-greater speed and luxury, whereas its economics actually show that progress in civil aviation is better measured by aircraft that will carry more passengers more cheaply (as Boeing's 747 quickly established). A new generation of smaller supersonic executive jets will soon once again challenge the exceptionalism conferred on the super-wealthy, whose upper-atmospheric carbon footprint will be proportionally larger than anybody else's apart from the military.

The fire that consumed R101 turned out to be a major nail in the coffin of airships' reputation. Anyone connected with Zeppelins had always carried at the back of their minds a constant awareness of how very dangerous hydrogen was as a lifting gas. The safe alternative was helium because it is inert, but it was unavailable in bulk in Europe. Helium in quantity had first been discovered beneath the United States' Great Plains as a component of natural gas before the First World War. For many years this gave America a virtual monopoly of the element. In 1925 the US Helium Act banned its export because the extent of this natural resource was still not known. As a consequence, Zeppelins and other airships like the R100 and R101 were condemned to use highly flammable hydrogen as their lifting gas while US naval airships were borne safely aloft by helium.

The *Graf* continued its flights and was received with celebrations everywhere. However, its last appearance in Chicago in October 1933 was noticeably cooler because now, to conform with a new Nazi law, the airship carried a vast swastika emblazoned on the tail. Dr Eckener, who despised Hitler and the new German government, was humiliated by this

requirement but had to obey. Still, he was cheered by the knowledge that back home the biggest and most luxurious Zeppelin ever to be built was taking shape: the LZ129, soon to be named *Hindenburg*. Hitler was not remotely interested in airships but he fully appreciated the *Graf*'s celebrity and hence the propaganda value of this new masterpiece of German technology.

Unlike that of its predecessor, the *Hindenburg*'s interior design was clean and modernist. The public rooms were spacious, with a separate lounge, dining room and reading room. There was even a smoking room, despite the presence overhead of more than 7 million cubic feet of hydrogen. This was made possible by the room having an airlock door and by allowing the bar steward alone to light passengers' cigars and cigarettes

The R100 was known as the 'capitalist' ship, having been built by private enterprise. Simply yet beautifully engineered, it was bigger even than the *Graf Zeppelin* and made a successful round trip to Canada. When airships fell out of favour it was scrapped for £450.

with a glowing car-type lighter. He also made sure that nobody carried their own matches or left the room with a lit cigarette. Apart from that, all the crew's catwalks and ladders leading to the gigantic bags of hydrogen were rubber-coated, and anyone whose maintenance job took them through such regions wore an asbestos suit without metal buttons. By such means, it was hoped, there could be no chance of sparks from static electricity. These, of course, were areas of the airship that passengers would not visit or need to know about. In their sumptuous domain, what with four toilets, a shower room and cabins all with hot and cold running water, a berth aboard the *Hindenburg* most closely resembled first-class travel on a liner like *Queen Mary*, and with prices to match.

The airship was duly launched and by the end of the 1936 season the *Hindenburg* had clocked up over 3,000 hours flying 1,600 transatlantic passengers in great comfort. What was more, wherever it went it acted as an unignorably vast advertisement for the might of German engineering, while the gigantic swastika on its tail associated that technology with the powerful new force of Nazism. This role had perhaps been at its most obvious when the 800-foot-long airship hung above the stadium in Berlin for the opening ceremony of the Olympic Games on 1 August 1936 and was thereafter on daily display, towing the Olympic banner. In the stadium below, the thousands of foreign spectators could not fail to be impressed by the massed ranks of impeccably uniformed and disciplined Party members of all ages while the symbol of aerial supremacy glided overhead.

◇◇◇◇◇◇◇◇◇◇◇◇◇◇◇◇◇◇◇◇◇◇◇◇

Meanwhile, the technology of ordinary commercial aircraft had been rapidly improving. Each day, airlines big and small were flying to thousands of destinations the world over. There was still no civil airliner capable of safely flying the North Atlantic without refuelling, but that would change within a couple of years. Otherwise, aircraft big and small were daily forging into ever-remoter interiors where previously communications had been intermittent. In the United States aviation had lapsed somewhat after its world-first start in 1903, paralysed by the Wright brothers' ludicrous attempt to patent any form of flight control in any aircraft, including foreign ones. This was so intimidating that after America joined the First World War in 1917 its only aircraft to see any real service was the excellent Curtiss JN-4 'Jenny', a biplane trainer. There were no American fighters or bombers. American pilots were obliged to fly French and British machines. Even as

The Boeing 247 airliner has been described as the first modern airliner, streamlined and with retractable landing gear. Sadly, it was exclusively produced for one airline, obliging competitors to turn to the Douglas DC-1 and its famously dominant successors.

late as 1925, it was no accident that Henry Ford would model his Trimotor too closely on the Fokker Trimotor. Ironically, the Dutch aircraft won the Ford Reliability Tour in that very year.

However, by the early 1930s the US aircraft industry had regained its mojo. Boeing's all-metal, low-wing 247 first flew in 1933 and set new standards of modernity. Apart from having retractable landing gear it even had an autopilot and inflatable rubber de-icing boots on the leading edges of its wings and tailplane. The comfort of its ten passengers was enhanced by air conditioning as well as soundproofing, not to mention soft seats and a stewardess bringing them drinks and meals from the tiny galley. With a cruising speed of almost 190 mph (306 kph) it was also fast enough to knock seven hours off the usual flight time between San Francisco and New York.

Simultaneously the Douglas Company's twin-engined and popular DC-2 was enlarged into the DC-3, which first flew in 1935. One might say this celebrated aircraft flew into the history books as arguably the most successful aircraft of all time, equally reliable as an airliner, a cargo plane or a military workhorse. Furthermore, it was the first aircraft that convinced airlines that carrying passengers could be profitable. Three years after its introduction it was carrying an astonishing 95 per cent of all US passengers and had already been sold to thirty foreign airlines. Douglas stopped making the DC-3 in 1947, by which time they had built 10,654 examples in a mere dozen years. Eighty-five years after it first flew, the DC-3 is still flying somewhere in the world today in one form or another, including in a

The Latécoère 521 of 1935 was designed for long-distance French empire routes. A luxurious flying boat, the Laté had 6 Hispano-Suiza engines (two in tandem) and was capable of a good turn of speed for so large an aircraft: 162 mph (261kph).

turboprop version for Antarctic work (the Basler BT-67). No other vehicle on land or sea could make the same commercial claim unless it was offering tourists self-consciously antiquarian 'heritage' rides.

In the mid-1930s the safety margin of flying was much improved by this new generation of all-metal twin-engined monoplanes because they were designed to fly on one engine if need be. Four-engined all-metal aircraft were in fact already flying even before *Hindenburg* first rose into the air at Friedrichshafen. Such aircraft made possible quite lengthy journeys over water as well as the ability to haul considerable amounts of freight. If one stresses the all-metal nature of their construction it is because there were still so many fabric-covered biplanes in service, like Imperial Airways' safe but antiquated Handley Page aircraft.

Nor had France been idle for it, like Britain, had an empire to service. The twin-engined, all-metal Bloch MB220 of 1935 was roughly equivalent to the DC-2, as was the Breguet 470. But the real challenge to transatlantic Zeppelins came from the new generation of all-metal seaplanes in France, Britain and the United States. The French Latécoère 521, also of 1935, was one of the first big, luxurious flying boats expressly designed for transatlantic service on the AfricaBrazil (Dakar to Natal) route. It could carry seventy-two passengers and had two decks, and contained a saloon with twenty armchairs and tables, a galley and a bar, and six deluxe double cabins, each with its own bathroom. Further development of French aircraft like these was abruptly curtailed by the Second World War.

Next spread: From 1936 Douglas's DC-3 became the most celebrated of all piston-engined airliners — rugged and adaptable, as famous in its military roles as in its civilian. Here it is seen in its military form as a C-47A in D-Day markings.

Imperial Airways began
flying its new fleet of
Short S23 Empire aircraft
in 1936. The one shown
here, *Cordelia*, was to
serve unscathed with the
RAF in the Second World
War and afterwards
resumed commercial
operations with BOAC
before being broken up
at Hythe in 1947.

As for Britain, in 1936 Short brought out a bigger version of the Calcutta for Imperial Airways. This was the Short Empire, which formed the basis of variant successors such as the military Sunderland that was to render remarkable service in the Second World War as a long-distance patrol and rescue flying boat. The Empire, as its name suggests, was designed for Imperial Airways' overseas routes that by now included a service to Australia. With large fuel reserves, four engines and a newly designed all-weather hull the Empire was fully equipped for long-distance transoceanic flights. In the summer of 1937 one flew from Ireland to Newfoundland even as one of the new American Sikorsky S-42 flying boats made the same journey in the opposite direction. The S-42 was to be followed in the late 1930s by the

Martin M-130 and the Boeing 314, all three flying boats becoming part of Pan American's famous 'Clipper' fleet flying long distances (such as down to Rio de Janeiro, or from California to Hawaii). It is to such flying boats in particular that people look back with what is today a largely imaginary nostalgia, for few still alive can have memories of flying on them.

Of these, the Boeing 314 Clipper has the reputation of being the most luxurious of them all. Pan Am's idea was to provide the very best for wealthy passengers needing to fly long distances. The big hull was configured for either seventy-four seats or forty sleeping berths. Those in sleepers enjoyed dressing rooms and a spacious lounge. In the onboard kitchen chefs prepared sumptuous meals, served in the dining salon by

Aboard a Sikorsky S-42 of Pan American's 'Clipper' fleet. Wood (or maybe Formica) panelling and comfortable chairs make for elegant modern travel. But note the watertight bulkhead door designed to be dogged shut to prevent flooding in an emergency.

Surely the most graceful of all piston-engined passenger aircraft, Lockheed's Constellation started life during the war as military transport. After 1945 it opened up intercontinental air routes, its elegant lines matched by the comfort it afforded its passengers.

uniformed waiters. In May of 1939 Pan Am began a transatlantic mail service in their fleet of Clipper 314s but four months later the outbreak of war in Europe put a stop to all that. The aircraft were used during the war to fly leaders like Churchill and Roosevelt to conferences, but by 1945 the era of the flying boat was at an end, such aircraft having been overtaken by newer and faster long-distance passenger models such as Lockheed's magnificent Constellation and the Douglas DC-6. Britain made a gallant – if ill-thought-out – post-war attempt to find a market for a new generation of big flying boats with their huge and technically advanced Saunders-Roe Princess. But war had changed the world, not least by leaving hundreds of new airstrips all over Africa and the Middle and Far East, making the ability to land on water very much less relevant. None of the three examples of the Princess sold, and after many years in mothballs they were broken up. It was a tragic miscalculation of the post-war market, as was the Bristol Brabazon, an equally unsellable giant airliner intended for a comparative handful of first-class passengers and destined for nothing more glamorous than the scrapyard.

A Pan Am poster from the 1960s, by which time the passenger was part of the Jet Age, flown in a Boeing 707 or a Douglas DC-8. The illustration is by Aaron Fine.

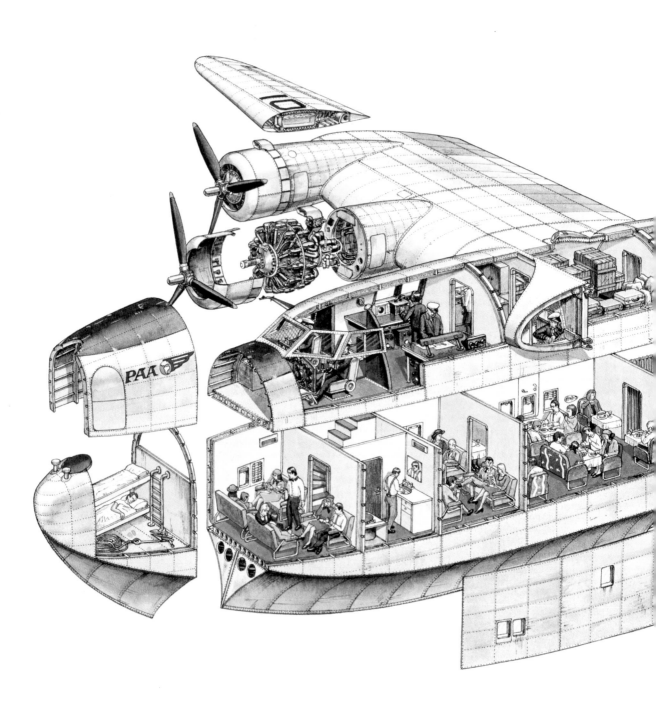

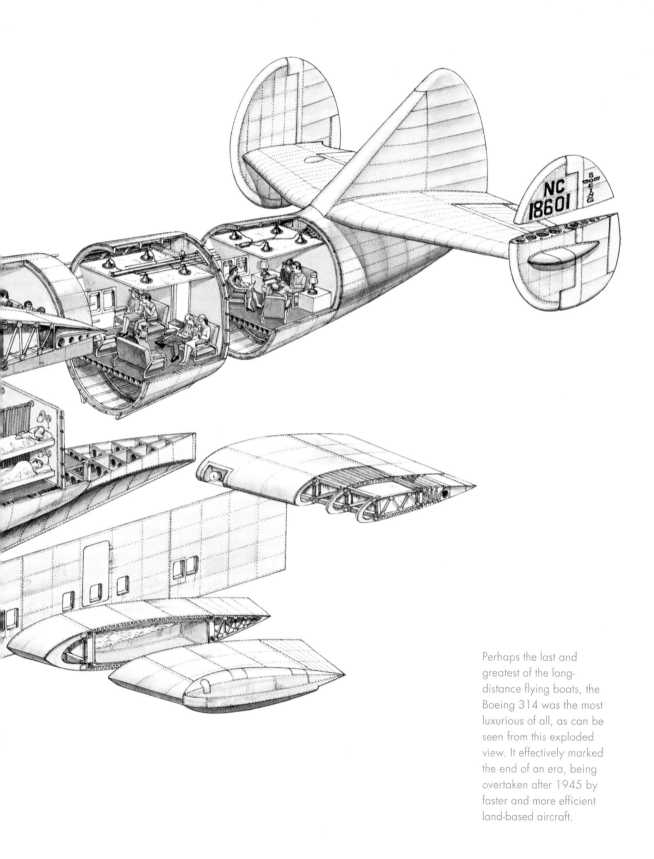

Perhaps the last and greatest of the long-distance flying boats, the Boeing 314 was the most luxurious of all, as can be seen from this exploded view. It effectively marked the end of an era, being overtaken after 1945 by faster and more efficient land-based aircraft.

Previous spread: The *Hindenburg*'s end at Lakehurst Naval Air Station, New Jersey, in May 1937. It was originally designed as a helium airship but the gas proved too expensive and difficult to source, and highly flammable hydrogen had to be used instead.

What the great pre-war flying boats offered their privileged passengers – in addition to considerable comfort – was the glamour of adventure at a time before flying became as humdrum as a bus ride. Even in the 1930s, backed up by four engines and the ability to land on water, setting off by air across the Pacific at an average speed of 170 mph (274 kph) was a technological challenge in those pre-radar days when navigation was still performed by dead reckoning. All three of Pan Am's handsome Martin M-130s would be lost to accidents by the end of the war. Living dangerously was all part of the spice of flying in those interwar years. As the French pioneer aviator Jean Conneau (aka André Beaumont) once remarked: 'Danger? But danger is one of the *attractions* of flight.' This is not a philosophy that would appeal in the timorous twenty-first century.

It is certain that such advances in aviation would anyway have brought to a close nearly four decades of Zeppelin history even without the *Hindenburg*'s dreadful fate. Like the sinking of the *Titanic*, this tragic episode is too well known to dwell on. Briefly, on the evening of 5 May 1937 and having crossed the Atlantic, the airship was over Lakehurst Naval Air Station in New Jersey. It had been delayed somewhat by stormy weather, and there had been a thunderstorm over the airfield that had only recently dissipated. In order to lose the last few hundred feet of altitude the *Hindenburg* vented off hydrogen and sank towards the mooring mast as the crew threw down the mooring ropes as usual. At that point observers on the ground noticed dancing blue sparks like flickers of St Elmo's fire along the airship's back and then beneath it. Suddenly a huge column of flame blossomed from the top of the hull and within seconds the airship's rear half became a roaring inferno. As the hydrogen in the huge gas cells caught fire the airship lost all remaining buoyancy and, its rear half reduced within seconds to a vast skeleton of Duralumin girders, it crashed to the ground almost on top of the scattering crowds. There is a famous recording of a radio reporter who was sent to cover what was supposedly a routine landing describing a scene that within seconds had become an inferno. Overcome with emotion as he realises he is witnessing a major tragedy, he can only blurt horrified phrases: 'Oh, the humanity… and all the passengers… a mass of smoking wreckage…' and he has to break off with stammered apologies.

When the debris had cooled and the bodies counted there were thirty-six dead and everyone was amazed that nearly two-thirds of those aboard the *Hindenburg* had somehow survived, although many with burns and other injuries caused by jumping. The R101's death toll had been higher, but the greater visibility of the giant Zeppelin and the presence of press photographers, reporters and a great crowd of horrified witnesses made its end far more potent in effect. It was a cruel irony, too, for never in over 2,300 commercial flights since 1910 had there been a single Zeppelin passenger fatality. For twenty-seven years, while carrying 50,000 passengers, the German airships had maintained an impeccable safety record. This was very much more than could be said for conventional aircraft over the same period, which had long been racking up a considerable death toll.

Opposite: A Martin M-130 'China Clipper' over San Francisco in 1935. Three M-130s ran a scheduled Pan American passenger service across the Pacific until 1945, by which time all had crashed. They were well appointed, with curtained couchette-style sleeping berths.

3

CARS

The car as we know it was a European invention, specifically German and French. The first vehicle to be driven by petrol rather than by steam was Karl Benz's of 1885, granted a patent the following year. The Benz Patent-Motorwagen he built in his workshop in Mannheim was a rear-engined motor tricycle that to modern eyes looks impossibly flimsy. Even so, in 1888 Benz's wife Bertha took her two boys in the car's third version and, apparently without her husband's knowledge, drove from Mannheim to Pforzheim to visit her mother, a distance of 65 miles (105 km). They had to stop en route to buy petrol from pharmacies but by evening they had arrived, and Bertha – the world's first woman car driver on the first long-distance drive – proudly sent her husband a telegram. The journey is still commemorated every two years by a rally for antique cars along her route. Benz went on to build the world's first production car, the Velo of 1894, and in the following year the first internal combustion-engined bus. By the end of the century Benz was among the world's biggest companies.

Karl Benz had bench-tested the world's first petrol engine in 1879, but it was not until 1885 that he made it power a vehicle. It was a single cylinder 4-stroke motor of 954 cc that gave his 'Motorwagen' three-quarters of a horsepower.

Also in 1885, some 58 miles (93 km) away from Mannheim, Gottlieb Daimler and his engineer friend Wilhelm Maybach had built the world's first petrol-engined motorcycle. True, with its wooden frame, wood-spoked wheels and stabilisers on either side it bore little resemblance to a motorised bicycle of the day, but they had built it more to test the engine than as a template for future designs. In many respects their Daimler-Maybach engine was much better than Benz's, being faster-revving, although it lacked the Benz's spark ignition. The partners soon became commercially successful and by 1890 were widely recognised as building the best available petrol engines. That year the company became the Daimler-Motoren-Gesellschaft or DMG. (Daimler and Benz would eventually merge in 1926. Well before then, Wilhelm Maybach and his son Karl founded a company to build aero engines in 1909 and their diesel and petrol engines went on to power Zeppelin airships and various First World War aircraft. This was one more early example of an increasing crossover between cars and aviation.)

In 1901 Maybach and Daimler were commissioned to build a car for a wealthy Austrian diplomat, Emil Jellinek, who was living in Nice. Jellinek was already an avid participant in the early motor races (the first proper motor race had been in 1894, from Paris to Rouen) and he was a great admirer of

A Daimler Straight 8 of 1947. The Daimler Motor Co. was an independent British company formed after buying the right to use the Daimler name from DMG in 1896. Until the 1950s Daimler held the Royal Warrant to supply cars to the British Monarch.

BY APPOINTMENT
MOTOR CAR MANUFACTURERS
TO H.M. KING GEORGE VI

The D A I M L E R "STRAIGHT-EIGHT"
8-PASSENGER
LIMOUSINE

DMG. The 35-horsepower car he ordered was to be called the 'Mercedes', Mercédès being the nickname of Jellinek's ten-year-old daughter. He was very particular about the car's specifications. Since most cars of the period tended to have a high centre of gravity and were prone to overturning on sharp bends, his car had to be wider, longer and lower, with its engine in front and mounted directly on a steel chassis instead of on bearers above a wooden one. This was revolutionary in its day; and in due course the car swept all before it at races in 1901, its radical improvements quickly being recognised and copied. It also had the first 'honeycomb' radiator and the first gate gear-change, and one might say the basic architecture of the modern car had at that moment jelled.

In 1902 DMG produced an upgraded version of the type, its name now established as Mercedes rather than DMG. The new car was the Mercedes Simplex which, in its powerful 60-horsepower version, effectively founded a new category: the race-bred luxury automobile. It quickly became a favourite of royalty and the wealthy – a market that was also soon to be catered for by Rolls-Royces, Daimlers and sundry other marques with pretensions to 'aristocratic' lineage, most of which were unfortunately doomed to disappear in the Depression of the 1930s. By comparison with today's cars they might show their age in terms of performance, but for sheer beauty of design and engineering finish the great luxury cars of the first forty years of the century remain for ever in a class of their own.

In passing, it may be worth noting with only slight surprise that royalty should have been so quick to embrace the motor car as a suitable mode of travel. Given centuries of glossy horses with nodding plumes and stately coaches with footmen perched behind, it is curious that any crowned head would favour being driven in a new-fangled machine that could not possibly have a pedigree longer than about fifteen years. Moreover, no matter how expensive the marque, the early cars were by no means wholly silent. They emitted abundant smoke and mechanical smells and were prone to breaking down, not to mention frightening the horses. Yet in 1898 the Prince of Wales – not yet Edward VII – was taken for a ride in an early Daimler and must have been impressed, for in 1900 he bought a Daimler 56C of his own (now in the museum at Sandringham). True, he had long had a reputation as a playboy and was in many ways progressive – as was his mother, Queen Victoria, who was interested in early mechanical novelties such as moving photography and sound recording. In any case, there was no reason why royalty should be any less seduced by novelty than anybody else. The Daimler the Prince of Wales bought was British-made in Coventry by a British company, the

Daimler Motor Co. This had the German name because when Frederick Simms first started his firm it made Daimler engines under licence. The Prince of Wales's purchase of the car (which was in fact a French design) began a tradition of the British royal family's state vehicles being Daimlers. This lasted until 1950 when a mechanical failure led them petulantly to switch to Rolls-Royce. Today, of course, Rolls-Royce Motor Cars – as a wholly owned subsidiary of BMW – is a German company.

Meanwhile in France car pioneers had also been busy with their own designs and engineering breakthroughs, and the development of the automobile was in full – if still technologically early – swing. Even before DMG's Mercedes was busy setting the standard of the luxury automobile, the French had been 'democratising' this new form of transport by producing a cheap and cheerful runabout for the middle-class driver. French car companies of the day, like many of their counterparts elsewhere, were often founded by a wealthy entrepreneur (or even playboy) with a partner who was a gifted engineer: one supplying the money and enthusiasm, the other a technical genius. Thus, before the turn of the century Émile Levassor and René Panhard were building cars and engines under licence from DMG and had patented the first modern transmission, which had a proper crankshaft in place of the ubiquitous belt drive. Likewise, the playboy Marquis de Dion and his engineer partner Georges Bouton produced the De Dion-Bouton Voiturette in 1899 that was designed for ordinary people rather than for the idle rich. So successful was this that by 1900 they were rivalling Benz as the world's biggest car company.

⬦⬦⬦⬦⬦⬦⬦⬦⬦⬦⬦⬦⬦⬦⬦⬦⬦⬦⬦⬦⬦⬦⬦⬦

Both Britain and America were a little slower off the mark in emulating the great strides that were being made in the car's development on the Continent. Britain's Herbert Austin produced his first car, a Wolseley three-wheeler, in 1895 – a full ten years after Karl Benz's. However, in 1900 he produced a Voiturette reliable enough to win a 100-mile trial race. In terms of quality, though, the best British cars before 1906 were Lanchesters. From 1896 the three Lanchester brothers had brought some original engineering skills to cars, particularly in transmission design, having been shocked by what they saw as deficiencies in the quality of the cars on the market. In 1902 they introduced pneumatic tyres and the world's first disc brakes on their car's front wheels, anticipating by many years what was to become the standard future braking system.

By 1904 the established Manchester engineer Henry Royce and the Hon. Charles Rolls, who owned a car dealership in London, had banded together to build a car of their own. Like the Lanchester brothers, they were unimpressed by the quality of most of the cars on the market and were determined to build a model worthier of their skills and taste. That year they produced a 10-horsepower car: an improved version of Henry Royce's prototype of the previous year. The men's new (and now hyphenated) partnership was reflected on the car's badge. Two years later in 1906 they exhibited their latest model at London's Olympia Car Show. Available in either a 40- or 50- horsepower version, their Silver Ghost set new standards for a luxury automobile. Engineering everywhere would of course move on, but very few marques were destined ever to rival Rolls-Royce cars in their silent running and superlative attention to detail.

Silver Ghosts would be made until 1926, over the years incorporating numerous improvements and built in many different styles that reflected the way in which quality cars of the day were marketed. Rolls-Royce, like Bentley and numerous other luxury marques in Britain, the US and the Continent, would typically sell a car as a complete chassis, leaving it up

The De Dion-Bouton Voiturette of 1899 was a major seller in the early car market because it was designed as a cheap runabout rather than as a prestige motor car for the wealthy.

to the buyer to arrange a coachbuilder to design a body to his taste. (This was a tradition that would last practically until the Second World War, and in the 1930s especially it resulted in some extravagantly modernistic and streamlined body shells.) Most car companies had deals with specific coachbuilders and would recommend them. In the First World War, Silver Ghosts were often armoured and turned into military staff cars. Some were even half-tracked for desert and off-road use. By then they had become famous for mechanical reliability, much of which was due to Henry Royce's magnificent six-cylinder, 7-litre side-valve engine. Of the model's many famous endorsers, none was more effective than that of Lawrence of Arabia, who wrote 'A Rolls in the desert is above rubies' after his Silver Ghost tender had tackled and surmounted the most extreme desert conditions.

No sooner had the two partners produced the Silver Ghost than Charles Rolls became seriously attracted to flying. In those early years of the century the idea of flight held a mystique even more potent than that of the automobile, and engineers in particular often took a lively interest in dreaming up designs for ever-lighter but more powerful aircraft engines. Like most people, Rolls was deeply impressed by Louis Blériot's first-ever crossing of the Channel in 1909. To him it was a clear indication of a new form of travel with enormous possibilities for the future, and he was soon enthusiastically taking flying lessons. Unfortunately, while he was piloting his Wright Flyer in an air display near Bournemouth in the summer of 1910, the machine broke up in the air and Rolls was killed. After a mere six years the company he had co-founded was bereft of his aristocratic flair and marketing savvy. Yet 110 years later his name lives on as an indissoluble part of one of the world's great engineering companies, now a brand name on thousands of jet engines daily flying passengers about the world – a source of aviation power that Rolls himself could never have imagined.

〰〰〰〰〰〰〰〰〰〰〰〰〰〰

Over in the United States, Henry Ford started a couple of companies that failed before he brought out a car he called his Model A in 1903. It had a top speed of 28 mph (45 kph), which for a road car in those days was speedy enough. (In Britain that same year the Motor Car Act raised the speed limit from 14 mph (23 kph) to 20 mph (32 kph) where – amazingly – it would remain until 1930.) The Model A's virtue was its toughness. Henry Ford had already decided that he had no interest in the luxury end of the car market. What he had accurately foreseen was the unlimited potential of cars designed

for ordinary working people, especially farmers in places where metalled roads were scarce and rugged reliability was at a premium. His Model N that followed in 1906 was a perfect expression of his thinking. It was a reliable, basic vehicle that in those days cost £125 (by comparison, a Rolls-Royce Silver Ghost in the same year would have set a buyer back £2,500 or $12,125). Ford's most famous success, of course, was with his Model T. This first went on sale in 1908 and was a vehicle so basic as to be positively spartan – although it was purposely designed so that owners who wanted something fancier could add their own accessories, some of which would strike today's motorist more as essentials than optional extras. The Model T came without windscreen wipers, speedometer or even doors. Among its chief merits were an extremely tough suspension and a largely unburstable engine.

In 1908 the Model T cost around $800, roughly equivalent to about $20,000 (or £15,800) in today's terms, so it was not cheap. However, by late the following year Ford had sold 10,000 of them and the price quickly dropped to $200. Within ten years Ford cars accounted for half the US market and on British roads Model Ts made up 40 per cent of all cars. How Henry Ford managed this is a familiar tale. If half his business flair was to have spotted the enormous American market for a true 'people's car' well before the eponymous Volkswagen and even as middle-aged people were still marvelling at the very idea of a 'horseless carriage', the idea of mass

Henry Ford's 4-cylinder Model N of 1906 was a decisive step towards his goal of a mass-produced utility vehicle. This particular example has been so tarted up for display as to belie its inventor's intentions. Headlamps and hood were optional extras.

The Ford Model T of
1908 – the first of some
15 million examples.
A true 'people's car'
that was basic and
rugged. Today's
concours examples give
the wrong impression.
Those featured in Mack
Sennett's Keystone Cops
films (1912–17) seem
more authentic.

production on a moving assembly line was the other half of his genius. The germ of this idea might not have been entirely his, but it was his personal ruthlessness that developed and brought it to maximum efficiency. By 1927 he had built some 15 million Model Ts, by which time the design had long been obsolete. To have concentrated on the same car for nearly twenty years struck many people (and all his competitors) as absurd – especially when over that period motor vehicles and a newly mobile society had changed radically. True, Rolls-Royce was still making Silver Ghosts until 1926, but at the bespoke end of the market there was much more scope for individuality with coachbuilders suiting individual customers with well-stuffed wallets. Besides, superlative engineering had its own, timeless quality that the discerning appreciated. It set them above ordinary folk, as the American company Pierce-Arrow had made a point of emphasising about its own cars since 1915.

Assembly line mass production may have been a groundbreaking innovation but it was also horribly destructive. At a stroke it meant that skilled workers were no longer essential. Almost anyone who could perform a simple repetitive task for an eight-hour work day could take part in building a car, just so long as they didn't lag behind the speed of the conveyor belt. It was skill-destroying as well as soul-destroying. It was also market-destroying, especially in Europe where the prices of American mass-production cars grossly undercut those of indigenous marques that were still partly being built by hand. This was exactly how Model Ts had made such inroads into the British market.

Being small and simple units, family-style utility cars lent themselves perfectly to such production methods, certainly when compared to upmarket marques requiring painstaking coachwork – and above all when compared to aircraft. At the end of the First World War, the overwhelming majority of aircraft were still biplanes with wooden frames and wood-ribbed wings covered in doped fabric. The accuracy with which these were built was critical to the way they flew, and the joiners and riggers and fitters who made them were highly skilled. During the war, they were often recruited from cabinet-making or furniture companies – even from firms making pianos and other musical instruments. Great experience went into selecting suitable woods and rejecting anything substandard, and vast forests of spruce were felled in Canada and the US to feed the Allied aircraft industry. Only in the 1930s and in the rush to re-arm could assembly-line methods be used to build aircraft, the majority of which by then were all-metal. Even so, they had become far more complex machines in the interim, and the skill levels of aircraft factory workers was generally of a different order from those churning out vehicles for the mass market or for the military. By the late 1930s the chassis and shells of even luxury cars were mostly metal even if skilled wood- and leather-work was still needed for the interiors and upholstery.

◇◇◇◇◇◇◇◇◇◇◇◇◇◇◇◇◇◇◇◇◇◇◇◇◇

By 1914, therefore, most cars fell into one of two categories: high-end luxury vehicles for the wealthy (e.g. the Rolls-Royce Silver Ghost) or modern conveyances for the common man who could afford them (e.g. Ford's Model T). The difference between these categories was further emphasised by the effort companies made to produce stylish vehicles. A car that looked good as well as performing well was almost inevitably from the luxury sector. It would not be until the late 1920s that properly trained industrial designers began moving companies away from the boxy 'utility' look that mass-market cars had inherited from Ford's Model T. The American automobile

This 1915 Pierce-Arrow Type 48B five-passenger tourer cost just under $5,000: a tidy sum at the time. The faired headlights were a company innovation while the right-hand drive persisted until the early 1920s. Pierce-Arrows were also chosen as presidential cars.

company Pierce-Arrow set a precedent in its 1915 advertising campaign by actively promoting beauty of design over that of mere mechanical function. According to its advertisements the Pierce-Arrow Model 36 was not just a successful machine, it was also 'a successful work of art, in the same way that a Sargent or a Saint-Gaudens is a successful work of art'.[1] The car was an example of 'beauty clothing utility.' In this way the Pierce-Arrow's image was that of 'class' and represented the opposite end of the market spectrum to that of the Model T.

In the thirty years of their existence motorised vehicles had already changed people's attitudes and expectations, just as mechanisation was about to change warfare itself and the way it was waged. The social attitudes most affected were probably those governed by traditional notions of distance and time. Traditionally, these had been measured in terms of walking, or travel on horseback or in a horse-drawn conveyance. Above all, this was true in the countryside where railway stations might be few and far between, although even trains had themselves brought about a revolution. Never before in human history had people anywhere needed to plan their days in terms of minutes. What brought about this radical change was the invention of the railway timetable. Before that, few country-folk would even have thought in terms of hours. Theirs was a largely clockless society where time was gauged by unconscious glances at the sun or with an ear cocked for a church bell.

Suddenly, though, motor vehicles of all kinds had shrunk distances and made the accurate timing of appointments and meetings relevant.

Overhead, airships and then aircraft were not only shrinking distance but were indifferent to the nature of the terrain below them – neither slowed by a range of hills nor halted by a river. Whether in transatlantic liners, in the air or on dry land, this was the thrilling new world characterised by ever-increasing speed in which the young mostly rejoiced while greybeards shook their heads and called it unnatural. Horses were predicted to go the way of the longbow – although in the event they were still to provide vital horsepower in the First World War. In Italy the youthful Futurists had spotted speed's artistic and political potential, while everywhere young mechanics and aspiring playboys alike were hooked on it, above all by the excitement and glamour of air shows and motor races. In both, deaths were frequent, whether of pilots, drivers or spectators. Drivers were impaled on their steering columns or thrown from their seats headfirst into trees, else they were trapped beneath their wrecked vehicle and burned alive when the petrol tank ruptured. Spectators flocked to motor races and air displays, claiming to pray that nobody would be killed that day while secretly hoping at least for some decent thrills and a spot of carnage at a safe distance. Hundreds at Bournemouth that day in 1910 must have watched Charles Rolls fall to his death and gone home thoughtful. From such poor broken bodies a pungent miasma of fate, speed and daring arose – such that their successors became surrounded by auras of public glamour, and by extension some of this rubbed off on the car brands they so recklessly drove.

Vauxhall's A Type – here an A12 with the company's trademark 'V' flutings on the bonnet – was capable of 100 mph (161 kph). It was a good example of how advanced the best car marques were just before the First World War.

One other pre-1914 British marque that acquired a reputation for producing luxury cars while also offering considerable performance was Vauxhall. The 3-litre A Type was beautifully engineered and in 1910, three months after Charles Rolls's untimely death, one became the first-ever 20-horsepower car to exceed 100 mph (161 kph). This must have made the Motor Car Act's 20 mph (32 kph) speed limit as absurd then to a proud Vauxhall owner-driver as today's 70 mph (113 kph) speed limit on British motorways must be for drivers of cars capable of 200 mph (322 kph). But in 1908 policemen with stopwatches would lurk behind trees on the dusty unmade road leading into Kingston-upon-Thames, hoping to catch 'scorchers' – as motorists exceeding the new 20 mph (32 kph) speed limit were popularly known.

◇◇◇◇◇◇◇◇◇◇◇◇◇◇◇◇◇◇◇◇◇◇◇◇◇◇

The Bentley 3-litre of 1921 was delivered as a running chassis and the customer could have the body made by the coachbuilder of his choice – whether for touring (like this one) or for racing.

Once the First World War was over it was wealthy playboys and their engineers who began to commission new variants of the luxury car – roadsters designed not only for effortless elegance but for speed and the look of awe-inspiring power. Their design was partly drawn from race-track versions (which often differed little beneath the external coachwork)

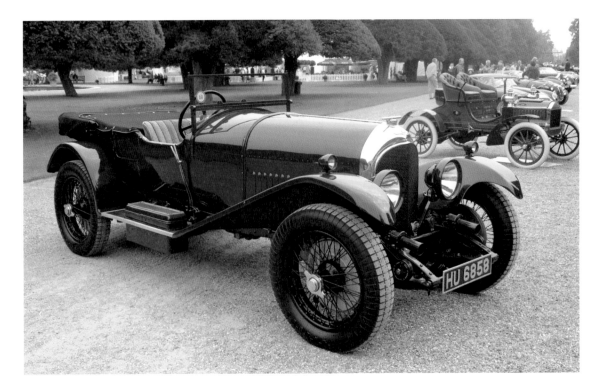

Bentley's massive 8-litre chassis was designed in 1930 not as a tourer but as a rich man's car for a body such as this one by Mulliner. The Depression was to make this the last Bentley before the company went bankrupt and was swallowed up by Rolls-Royce.

and partly from the great mechanical advances that had been made during the war in the design of aero engines. Generally speaking, the longer the car's bonnet or hood, the bigger and more potent its engine was assumed to be – and usually was. Such cars swiftly took on the glamour of their drivers at races while becoming an essential ingredient of newspaper stories, Hollywood films and adventure fiction. Walter Bentley was one such; essentially a racing driver more interested in a car's brute performance than in its stateliness, although with an excellent eye for the right 'look'. So perfectly did his 3-litre car of 1921 fit the bill that a band of rich playboys quickly bought one. They soon became known in the newspapers and cinema newsreels as 'the Bentley Boys' and they regularly gathered at places like the famous banked track at Brooklands.

Their doyen was the larger-than-life Woolf Barnato, massively wealthy from his family's South African diamond and gold mines and widely known for his quite extraordinary all-round proficiency in various sports. A list of the activities at which Barnato excelled would have disgraced Superman. In addition to being a world-class driver he also raced speedboats, boxed, was an outstanding amateur tennis player, bred horses, shot, and hunted to hounds while also playing first-class cricket for Surrey. Almost anything Woolf Barnato did was faithfully recorded by the newspapers, whose compositors must have had phrases like 'playboy', 'death-defying' and 'his latest exploit' already set up in large type, surrounded by thickets of exclamation marks. All this plus huge personal wealth led Barnato in

BM·1930

Previous spread: Frank Clement and Woolf Barnatto in a Bentley Speed Six in 1930. A child in a toy car sits beside them. From 1928 the 6.5-litre Speed Six was Bentley's tuned-up version for racing. After Woolf Barnato's memorable race across France in 1930 the type became widely known as the 'Blue Train' Bentley.

Below: The Bugatti Type 41 Royale was probably the largest and grandest of the interwar cars. Designed almost exclusively for deserving royalty, its 12.763-litre engine and over 3-tonne weight are somehow summed up by the radiator cap's trumpeting elephant.

due course to become Bentley's chairman, in which role he oversaw the production of a series of cars that have long since become collector's items. His Bentleys' bonnets did indeed grow progressively longer, climaxing in 1930 with a prodigious 8-litre car deliberately designed to outdo Bugatti's 13-litre Royale. One of Barnato's more famous exploits came that year when he bet £100 that not only could he beat the French *Train Bleu* express from Cannes to Calais in his 6.5-litre Bentley Speed Six, but he would be in London before the train had even reached Calais. He won by three-quarters of an hour which, given the time lost in crossing the Channel – not to mention stopping for petrol – was an impressive achievement.

This was the great age of extravagant cars that were beautifully engineered and shamelessly designed for daredevil driving. The spirit was perfectly captured in popular fiction such as Leslie Charteris's early 'Saint' stories, where his hero Simon Templar shares all and more of Woolf Barnato's Superman talents. The cars he drives have fictitious names like 'Hirondel', 'Desurio' and 'Furillac' – leaving the reader to imagine their real-life counterparts. His 'huge cream and red Hirondel' is described as a two-ton, eight-cylinder car that blows a gallon of petrol into smoke every three or four miles. In a 1930 novel, The Saint twice has to drive this car from London to the East Anglian coast to rescue his girlfriend and avert global disaster. A modern reader must take into account the narrow, unlit

and often poorly surfaced rural roads of ninety years ago where the less technically advanced tyres of the time frequently punctured, and when top speeds, acceleration and braking distances were considerably inferior to those of today. At first Simon Templar drives with relaxed skill, 'his lean brown hands seeming merely to caress the wheel of the Hirondel and his mad, mocking eyes lazily skimming the road that hurtled towards them at seventy miles an hour. He touched a switch, and the tremendous twin headlights slashed a blazing pathway for them through the darkness. And the big car roared out into the east.' Later in the book he makes the same journey but now against the clock, fretting at his progress. His former insouciant skill has been supplanted by the recklessness of a man competing at Brooklands, his co-driver now Mr Toad. Heaven help any ordinary motorist who happened to be pottering along the same road in his Baby Austin. 'Figures blazed through his brain in an ordered spate – figures on the speedometer of the Hirondel, trembling past the hair-line in the little window where they showed – seventy-five – eighty – eighty-five... Driving as only he could drive, with the devil at his shoulder and a guardian angel's blessing on the road and on the tyres, he might average a shade over fifty...'[2]

A plausible model for his Hirondel might be the Hispano-Suiza H6C. Originally a Spanish company founded at the end of the nineteenth century, Hispano-Suiza soon acquired a truly brilliant Swiss engine designer, Marc Birkigt. In the First World War, Birkigt designed a revolutionary lightweight cast-block aluminium V8 aero engine that was soon powering almost half of all Allied aircraft. As soon as the war was over, Hispano-Suiza returned to making luxury cars, their engines now incorporating many of the advances made by the company's aero engines. They introduced Birkigt's new H6 at the 1919 Paris Salon and it created a sensation, being seen as the one marque that could take on and even beat Rolls-Royce for sheer quality of engineering. Not only that, but the H6 was much more powerful than practically any other quality roadster available at the time, including the now outdated Silver Ghost, and on all counts it was the more arresting piece of machinery. Rightly or wrongly, Hispano-Suiza saw itself in direct competition with Rolls-Royce for refinement and innovative engineering, and some of its patents (such as for power brakes) were actually used under licence by the British company. The H6's mechanical sophistication was such that one example was driven on a round trip from Paris all the way down to Nice and back without the driver having to add either water or oil – an unheard-of feat in those days when spare cans of petrol, oil

and water (and often two spare tyres) were usually carried as a matter of course on any journey longer than 50 miles (80 km) or so. Birkigt was nominated for Car Engineer of the Century for his magnificent H6, but he equally deserved a medal for his aero engines that during the war had powered some of the most significant Allied aircraft, including the French SPAD VII and XIII as well as the Sopwith Dolphin and the British Aircraft Factory's excellent S.E.5A, one of the war's fastest fighters. Not only that but Birkigt also turned out to be a brilliant weapons designer, notably of the 20 mm cannon that was to become the RAF's standard weapon in the Second World War.

One H6 that preserved the tight links between aviation and automobiles was built in 1924. This was commissioned by André Dubonnet, an accomplished pilot and racing driver who was also heir to the famous aperitif company. The coachwork of his H6C was entirely of tulipwood and was built by one of the First World War's greatest aircraft companies, Nieuport. The car is known as the 'Tulipwood Torpedo' and still exists – a gorgeously polished example of the coachbuilder's art.

The H6 that Hispano-Suiza produced in the early 1920s had a big straight-

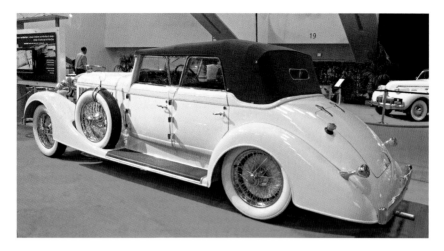

A 1928 Hispano-Suiza H6C convertible sedan. Swiss engineering combined with French artistic flair. This particular car was intended for the US market yet all the French-built examples were right-hand drive. Its weight limited it to a top speed of 90 mph (145 kph).

six engine that was expanded to 8 litres in 1924. That year Woolf Barnato, the archetypal Bentley Boy, drove a Hispano-Suiza H6 to eight international records, including 300 miles (483 km) of the banked Brooklands track in Surrey at an average of 92 mph (148 kph). If such a car with a flamboyant touring body could have been the inspiration for The Saint's 'Hirondel' in 1930, the chances are it would not have been open like the Tulipwood Torpedo. By that time tastes were gravitating away from the open, racing car style so favoured by the Bentley Boys who were content to drive in all weathers wearing goggles and with most of the car's upholstery covered

Specially ordered for the 1924 Targa Florio race, Hispano-Suiza's Tulipwood Torpedo body was built on an H6C chassis using strips of what may actually have been mahogany and thousands of brass rivets for a bodyweight of a mere 160 pounds (72.5 kg).

by a drumming canvas tonneau. Now there was a growing preference for closed sedans or saloons. The added coachwork of steel and glass naturally added a good deal to the car's weight, but engines were becoming more powerful even as chassis and suspension became more sophisticated and resilient.

◇◇◇◇◇◇◇◇◇◇◇◇◇◇◇◇◇◇◇◇◇◇◇◇

All this while, American car manufacturers were building machines to rival anything in Europe. By 1923 Ford's Model T had changed little since its inception and – like Rolls-Royce's Silver Ghost – was something of an antique. Henry Ford was finally persuaded that an entirely new car was necessary and his new Model A was designed. However, in order for his factories to tool up to build it he had to close the lot simultaneously for six months, since they were all making the Model T. This handed his chief rival, General Motors, a huge advantage that some historians believe Ford never entirely overcame. GM was run by Alfred P. Sloan, a man who was easily Henry Ford's equal for sheer charmlessness – although, unlike Ford, he never sent Adolf Hitler an annual birthday cheque for $20,000 in the 1930s as a token of his admiration.* On the other hand, when GM's German subsidiary Opel was progressively Nazified after 1933 and purged of its Jewish employees, Sloan raised no objection.[3] By 1939 GM was the world's largest corporation.

Sloan's business model was the polar opposite to that of Henry Ford. Instead of selling a single product until it became obsolete, he favoured the idea of rapid obsolescence. Having discovered that on average his factories' machine tools needed replacing every two to three years, he decided the way forward was to produce a new model every two to three years, each incorporating the latest technological innovation. Not only that, his plan was to build five marques of GM car in ascending order of quality and cost. The entry-level car was a Chevrolet; then came Pontiac, Oldsmobile, Buick and lastly Cadillac as the top-of-the-range product. Moreover, each type was to be easily recognisable on the road, Sloan's idea being that GM customers, in their aspiration to drive the best they could afford, would trade upwards every two or three years and that everyone could see they were doing so.

Cadillacs had long been recognised as luxury cars on a par with any European equivalent. As early as 1912 a Cadillac came with an electric

---

* The admiration was mutual. In 1938 the German Consul in Cleveland awarded Ford the Grand Cross of the German Eagle.

starter that in theory put an end to the need for a capped and gauntleted chauffeur labouring away at a starting handle on cold mornings, while 'the quality' took their seats and fidgeted impatiently. In 1928 Cadillacs introduced partially synchromesh gears (the world's first all-synchromesh transmission would come in 1933 with the British Alvis 14.75 saloon). The previous year saw the introduction of the Cadillac LaSalle with a powerful V-8 engine. On one occasion such a car was driven for 952 miles (1,532 km) at an average speed of 95.2 mph (153.2 kph), which contrasted favourably with Woolf Barnato's record in the Hispano-Suiza three years previously. It is not inconceivable that a Cadillac LaSalle, new in 1927, might have

Above: In 1912 Cadillac became the first manufacturer to market a car with an electrical system that powered a starter, ignition, lights and horn. In particular, the self-starter was a revolutionary departure at the time and must have seemed a wonderful innovation.

Left: Cadillac's 1927 LaSalle was intended to compete against the Packard 6 and was given a new and powerful V-8 engine. Its style was inspired by Hispano-Suiza, and its comparatively high price counted against it after the Wall Street Crash of 1929.

La Nouvelle Arrivée

FAVORITE—IN SMART CIRCLES EVERYWHERE

Wherever you go, you will find the La Salle the pronounced favorite in the smarter, more discriminating circles. The reason is plain. The more one appreciates charm of contour and of color, and values the finer points of motor car performance, the higher is the La Salle esteemed. The powerful appeal of the La Salle lies in the surpassing degree in which it combines unique style and exquisite beauty, with performance so smooth, so brilliant, as to be a continuous source of gratification and delight. Only a car upon which has been lavished the finest workmanship of Fisher Body craftsmen, and which enjoys the engineering supremacy of the 90-degree, V-type, 8-cylinder engine design, could approach so near complete and detailed perfection

You may possess a LaSalle on the liberal term-payment plan of the General Motors Acceptance Corporation—the appraisal value of your used car acceptable as cash

CADILLAC MOTOR CAR COMPANY
DIVISION OF GENERAL MOTORS CORPORATION
DETROIT, MICHIGAN   OSHAWA, CANADA

LA SALLE
FROM $2495 TO $2685 F.O.B. DETROIT

MANUFACTURED - COMPLETELY - BY - THE - CADILLAC - MOTOR - CAR - COMPANY - WITHIN - ITS - OWN - PLANTS

inspired Leslie Charteris's fictional 'Furillac' in some of his early novels that just pre-dated the 'Saint' series and whose heroes were well in the mould of the Barnato-style playboy with the skills of a racing driver.

The third car Leslie Charteris had Simon Templar drive was a 'Desurio'. This invention might possibly have been inspired by another great American marque of the period: the Duesenberg. In terms of top speed, many Duesenbergs would be considered respectably fast even today, while certainly not lagging at all in terms of cost. In 1933 Duesenberg produced their S. J. Arlington Torpedo Sedan that could reach an astounding 130 mph (almost 210 kph). This was soon known as the 'Twenty Grand' from its then-astronomical price of $20,000. As a comparison: other prestige American marques of the day – Cord, Marmon, Cadillac, Auburn, Pierce-Arrow, Stutz – were mostly priced at around $3,000.

Opposite: With its European vignettes, Cadillac's poster for their new LaSalle conjured up chic international travel.

Above: Duesenberg's Model J was a favourite of film stars in the early 1930s. It was sensationally fast and sensationally expensive. The 'ordinary' version managed 94 mph (151 kph) in second gear and the supercharged Model SJ (as in this Arlington Torpedo) could reach 140 mph (225 kph).

Next page: Barley's Roamer was introduced in 1916 and in 1918 acquired a 75-h.p. Duesenberg engine. In 1921 a Roamer set six speed records at Daytona Beach. Like so many other car companies, Barley went out of business in 1929.

The ROAMER

America's Smartest Car

The Duesenberg "miracle motor" now adds time and distance mastery to *Roamer* design distinction. Seventy-five miles an hour on the straightaway and fifty miles an hour over hills is guaranteed.

Duesenberg motors have driven over 50% of America's fastest racing cars; and now, in the new *Roamer*, for the first time in motor car history, the Duesenberg motor is obtainable.

A bettered body design; a sturdier, stronger, light-weight chassis frame; deft aristocracies such as individual steps; tonneau windshield; rakish fenders; backs and cushions of rich, thick, genuine leather; padded top — these, together with the purchaser's own option of body finish,

color, top material and upholstery, distinguish the new Duesenberg-motored *Roamer*; and the complete equipment includes, besides many expected things, a Bosch magneto, a sylphon thermostat, wire wheels and Goodyear cord tires.

The *Roamer* Six, Duesenberg-motored, with seven-passenger body, and the *Roamer* Four, Duesenberg-motored with four- and seven-passenger bodies, may be seen at the National Automobile Shows.

Also a new type *Roamer* Six with an improved Continental motor, in four- and seven-passenger body styles.

BARLEY MOTOR CAR COMPANY, *Kalamazoo, Michigan*

Above: A 1912 Stutz Bearcat. That year Bearcats won twenty-five of the thirty races they entered. Note the 'monocle' windshield clipped to the steering column.

Below: This 'pimp my auto' styling of an Auburn 851 speedster is a tribute to the coachworker's art, if not to the owner's taste.

The Henri Chapron model of Delahaye's 1937 V-12 was a superlative example of French engineering and styling. It was also very fast, being capable of 143 mph.

Apart from Hispano-Suizas, equivalent European luxury-class race-bred cars of the 1930s included such French types as Bugatti, Delage and Delahaye; the British Bentley, Invicta, Aston Martin and Lagonda; the German Mercedes, BMW and Auto Union; and the Italian Alfa Romeo, Lancia and Isotta Fraschini. One American enthusiast's recent judgement is that, 'If you want supercars in the 1930s you *can* only choose Delahaye, Delage and Cord. If you want hypercars or luxury supercars of the period, you *can* only choose Duesenberg.' But champions of machinery, no matter whether speedboats, motorbikes, aircraft, cars or even lawn mowers, are often extravagantly – even belligerently – opinionated.

Cord's 810 of 1930 was styled by Gordon Buehrig, who also styled for Stutz, Duesenberg and Auburn. The distinctive coffin nose and pop-up headlights concealed less visible innovations.

Right: Invicta was – and perhaps still is – a British car company that from its first model in 1925 to its latest in 2012 suffered at least four bankruptcies. Invicta's 4.5 litre S-Type was produced between 1931 and 1935.

Below: The Delage D8 120 Super Sport first appeared at the Paris Motor Show in 1937. With its 120-h.p. engine it was an excellent example of a French car designed for the luxury end of the market.

Previous spread: A 2-litre Lagonda in its 'Speed' variant temporarily fails to live up to its name in a race at Brooklands. When not bulldozing sand, this model of the late 1920s with the big front brake drums was easily capable of 80 mph.

From 1937 onwards BMW's light and nimble 2-litre 328, with its top speed of 103 mph, was a winning design. In 1945 its captured plans heavily influenced the design of both the Bristol 400 and Jaguar's XK 120.

The 1936 Auto Union C was a milestone in racing cars with its wind-tunnel tested profile and its massive V-16 engine placed behind the driver. This engine was so powerful it was possible to spin the wheels at 150 mph and led to the car's notorious handling problems. But when mastered, the C won a lot of pre-war races.

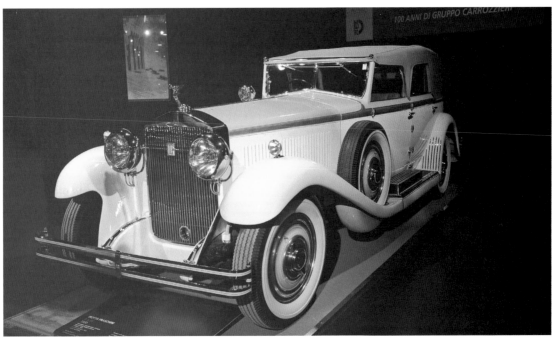

By the early 1930s most upmarket cars were closed, and for sheer over-the-top magnificence it would be hard to outdo Ettore Bugatti's Type 41, the Royale. This was just the sort of car that The Saint would have scorned as far too regal for a man of action, just as James Bond would never in a million years have chosen to drive a Rolls. Piqued by someone saying that Bugatti couldn't produce anything to rival a Rolls-Royce, Ettore produced a three-ton monster with a 12.75-litre engine that is still one of the world's largest-ever cars. Only seven were built, one of which Ettore himself wrote off when he fell asleep at the wheel. Another he point-blank refused to sell to King Zog of Albania on the grounds that 'the man's table manners were beyond belief'.[4] With admirably rigid social standards like that it is perhaps small wonder that so many remarkable car marques went out of business in the Depression years. There is no doubt that in its mechanical sophistication and astonishingly good handling for a car that heavy, the Royale was an entirely plausible rival to Rolls-Royce. It certainly had beautiful lines with a prodigiously long bonnet, and the enormous sweep of its front mudguards to a running board that, for the chauffeur in front, was still tilted at a slight angle.

However, from the late 1920s there was an increasing sense among some of the more progressive car manufacturers that sheer size and splendour were no longer enough. For a really up-to-date look a car ought to be streamlined as though moulded by the very wind of its own passing – exactly what the Bentley Boys' cars were not (Ettore Bugatti once disparaged them as 'the world's fastest lorries'). Such a change of aesthetic accorded with the new fashion for streamlining that will be noted further in the chapter on trains and has already been explored in some detail in the Introduction, where mention was made of early Italian examples of teardrop-shaped vehicles such as the advanced Alfa Castagna Aerodinamica of 1913. Now architects like Le Corbusier and industrial designers such as Norman Bel Geddes produced all sorts of aerodynamic data deriving from wind tunnel tests to show that the ideal streamlined shape was indeed that of a teardrop, with the greater mass in front.

This was not exactly news in the highly specialised world of land speed record-setting. In the previous chapter a brief mention was made of the 1929 world record set by Henry Segrave in his Napier *Golden Arrow*. In reality, from the moment in 1925 when Malcolm Campbell had achieved 150.87 mph (242.8 kph) in his Sunbeam, the world land speed record became a virtually unchallenged British monopoly until the Second World War. By 1935 Campbell had raised the record to 301.129 mph (484.62 kph) in his Campbell-Railton Blue Bird. This was a beautifully sleek machine, powered

Opposite top: To meet a new 3-litre race formula, Auto Union developed their D type in 1937. With the lighter V-12 engine and swing axles, the car's handling was a great improvement on that of its predecessor.

Opposite bottom: The Italian luxury marque Isotta Fraschini produced fewer than a thousand completed chassis of their 8A model between 1924 and 1931. The 7.3 litre straight-8 engine was the most powerful of its type in the world.

Perhaps the first of the record-breakers to be properly streamlined, the Irving-Napier *Golden Arrow* enabled Henry Segrave to break the land speed record at 231.45 mph (372.48 kpm) in March 1929 at Daytona Beach.

(as all such cars were) by an aero engine – in this case the Rolls-Royce R Type that had enabled Britain to retain the Schneider Trophy for racing floatplanes and was the direct antecedent of the Merlin engine. Thereafter Malcolm Campbell retired and the record became disputed between George Eyston's Thunderbolt and John Cobb's Railton Special. In August 1939 the Railton, powered by two Napier Lion aero engines, raised the record to 369.74 mph (595.04 kph). Its beautifully streamlined shell was the perfect embodiment of the ideal that industrial designers like Le Corbusier and Bel Geddes envisioned. After the war, John Cobb further improved his Railton Special and in 1947 became the first to break the 400 mph (644 kph) barrier.

John Cobb's Railton Special outside the company works at Brooklands in 1938. It still lacks the bubble fairings over the wheels but its polished 'teardrop' profile is the apotheosis of the streamlined shape that industrial designers had long idealised.

Thunderbolt, in which George Eyston vied with John Cobb for the land speed record in the late Thirties. In 1938 Thunderbolt held the record for a year at 357.50 mph (575.34 kph) until Cobb won it back. With the car's elongated shape and weight of 7 tons the stabilising fin was crucial.

Similar streamlining was also employed in Germany for record-breaking just before the war. That country's Mercedes-Benz and Auto Union *Silberpfeile* ('silver arrows') completely dominated motor racing in the 1930s and their know-how translated easily into cars for record-breaking on Germany's new autobahns. In 1938 the German racing driver Rudolf Caracciola took the Mercedes-Benz W125 to a speed of 269 mph (433 kph): a record that still stands as the highest speed achieved on a public road. His Rekordwagen had a highly streamlined shell not unlike Cobb's Railton Special. Dr Ferdinand Porsche designed its successor, the six-wheeled T80. With its stub wings to provide downforce this was even more futuristic-looking, but it was destined never to try for a new record. It was powered by a 44.5-litre Daimler-Benz aircraft engine that, once war had broken out, was summarily reclaimed by the Luftwaffe. The car itself can still be seen in the Mercedes-Benz Museum in Stuttgart.

The Mercedes 540K of 1938 had a supercharged straight-8 engine, giving this powerful tourer a top speed of well over 100 mph.

Above: In some ways the most aesthetically pleasing of the speed record breakers, the Campbell-Railton Blue Bird was the first to break 300 mph (483 kph), achieving 301.129 (484.62 kph) mph on the Bonneville Salt Flats, Utah, in September 1935.

Below: In 1939 Dr Ferdinand Porsche aimed his six-wheeled Mercedes-Benz T80 at a new land speed record of 466 mph (750 kph). It was powered by a hugely uprated Messerschmitt Bf.109 engine of 44.5 litres. The war came and the car never ran, but it can be seen in the Mercedes Museum in Stuttgart.

Back in the 1930s America of mass-produced cars, Norman Bel Geddes, who as a keen sailor was fascinated by water, waves and the best shape for a hull, insisted that 'Speed is the cry of our era, and greater speed one of the goals of tomorrow.'[5] But that was theory; in practice the executives of car companies were not so easily convinced of the ideal teardrop shape for automobiles, principally for two good reasons. In the first place implementing this sort of radical design would require very expensive factory re-tooling; and in the second, they were by no means certain the public would buy the idea or the product. Their cautiousness about their customers' innate conservatism was well borne out by the reception given to General Motors' Chrysler Airflow in 1934, whose advertisement was quoted in this book's Introduction. The copy disingenuously implied that its designers had been inspired by 'mother nature': 'You have only to look at a dolphin, a gull, or a greyhound to appreciate the rightness of the tapering, flowing contour of the new Airflow.' But the truth was that the Airflow had not been designed either by naturalists or by professional stylists like Bel Geddes or Gordon Buehrig. It was the product of an in-house team at Chrysler. Despite claims of its 'tapering, flowing contour' the car looked neither light nor speedy. With the small, high windows that made its sides seem unnaturally tall it more resembled a black beetle in its heavy, slightly armoured appearance and looked not a bit like a dolphin, a gull or a greyhound. Add to that an engine that was unreliable, and not surprisingly the Chrysler Airflow failed to sell.

Late in 1935 Ford introduced its Lincoln-Zephyr which, by contrast, got its streamlined aerodynamics absolutely right. Its designer, Eugene Gregorie, had started out designing yachts; and in the Lincoln-Zephyr's backward-raked and sleekly pointed radiator it is not hard to see a speedboat's bows. New York's Museum of Modern Art called the Lincoln-Zephyr 'the first successfully streamlined car in America', an accolade presumably referring to mass-produced cars rather than to the bespoke market, where extravagantly windswept designs were already commonplace.

American cars in general had long tended to be larger than their European counterparts, and in the late 1930s mass-produced Fords and Buicks and Hudsons often rivalled upmarket European marques in terms of size and mechanical sophistication. One reason for bigger cars in the US was that cities tended to be further apart than in Europe. Being bigger also made them seem more luxurious, especially as seen through the lenses of Hollywood. Nor was economical performance quite so pressing since America was self-sufficient in oil and miles per gallon was seldom a deciding factor in choosing a car. As quite ordinary American car engines became steadily bigger the phrase 'gas-guzzling' came to be used sniffily as well as enviously by Europeans, with the implied and quite misplaced criticism that, weight for weight, US engines tended to be less mechanically efficient and sophisticated because 'they could afford to be'. After the war, as the new Jet Age took hold of designers' imaginations, pre-war streamlining morphed into styles that reflected supersonic aerodynamics. For the next two decades the blissful extravagances of wildly chromed fins and intakes that came to be known as 'Detroit baroque' dominated most American car design.

Ford's Lincoln-Zephyr. From its launch in 1936 New York's MoMA acclaimed it as 'the first successfully streamlined car in America', presumably referring only to mass-produced cars. Headlights have now taken as standard Pierce-Arrow's idea of twenty years earlier.

A Mercedes W154 in its 1938 configuration. Highly successful both before and after the war, the design epitomised how a racing car should look until John Cooper re-started Auto Union's pre-war rear-engined revolution that became the pattern for racing cars from the late 1950s.

4

TRAINS

Steam locomotion was invented in Britain in the first years of the nineteenth century and remained the majority form of mechanised land transport almost everywhere for the next 120 years. At first it had very mixed reviews in Britain. Younger people tended to see the growing rail network as a sign of progress, opening up the country and providing a faster and more comfortable alternative to horseback (or stagecoach) travel over roads that were seldom all-weather surfaced or 'metalled'. Older people often thought any form of travel that was faster than a horse unnatural and even irreligious. The famous objection of artists and intellectuals like John Ruskin was both moral and aesthetic, holding as he did that the railway was 'the loathsomest form of devilry now extant… destructive of all wise social habit and natural beauty'.[1]

J. M. W. Turner's celebrated *Rain, Steam and Speed* of 1844. A powerful image in its day as it depicted – or predicted – a brave new world. Its exact significance remains enigmatic, as does that of the putative hare.

It is more difficult to decide what the artist whom Ruskin championed, J. M. W. Turner, meant by his famous 1844 painting, *Rain, Steam and Speed*. Experts seem agreed that the train is crossing Maidenhead Bridge, heading away from London on Brunel's Great Western Railway. Despite Turner's famously impressionistic style, they also see a hare running along the track ahead of the train. What no one can agree on, however, is what this symbolises. Does it represent Ruskin's panicked and fragile natural world fleeing noisy and polluting machinery? Or might it rather show evidence of mankind's inventive genius forging unstoppably ahead into an industrialised future? Apparently Turner left no word on the matter. However, since the engine in the picture is heading towards the viewer, maybe the painter had the unconscious thought that the whole mechanised human race was going west – an ancient metaphor for death.

Others who objected to the railways were landowners who did not want their immemorial property bisected by a line that would become a de facto right of way to all and sundry, and in perpetuity. This was especially alarming in hunt country. The legacy of their stubbornness is still to be seen in Britain's rail network in the form of curves and detours that make little apparent sense today, but at the time were agreed in deference to landed gentry, many of whom sat in the House of Lords. It remains one of the reasons why straight high-speed lines often prove so hard to build. Nevertheless, the Victorian rail network spread rapidly amid market bubbles and collapses, bankruptcies suffered and fortunes made. By the turn of the twentieth century rail travel throughout Britain as well as on the Continent, in the United States and elsewhere had become the backbone of commercial and social life.

Well before then, one particular category of maximally luxurious rail travel had become established in most countries and states that had a monarchy. In 1842 Queen Victoria was the first British monarch to make use of a Royal Train, and the reason for her preferring to use it was presumably the same as that of her fellow royals in Europe. Compared with road travel at the time, rail travel was very much faster, smoother and more comfortable than travelling by road in a royal coach pulled by horses. Speed also gave one privacy and insulation from cheering crowds – not to mention wayside assassins. Not only was there space for a proper bedroom and a dining room but it was possible to hold meetings with ministers or secretaries at which proper minutes could be taken. Writing legibly in a horse-drawn coach was a skill few ever acquired.

In 1900 the Prince of Wales (shortly to become Edward VII) bought a

Daimler car, thus beginning the association of the marque with British royalty. From then onwards the growing sophistication of the internal combustion engine might have been seen as presaging a challenge to the railways. Yet for hauling immense loads of freight and passengers long distances, steam locomotives were to prove uniquely capable until the Second World War. After that, steam was generally replaced by electric, diesel-electric and other forms of motive power. As for rail transport itself, it remains today a major pillar of the global economy for both passengers and freight. Currently there are plans for a regular container service between Hamburg and Beijing that will take a mere seven days – vastly quicker than by sea.

Building the Transcontinental railway across the United States. This began in the mid-1860s and was initially hampered by the Civil War, and engines and materials having to be shipped to the West Coast via Cape Horn and Panama.

The Trans-Siberian Railway under construction some time after 1891. The world's longest line became a vast network connecting parts of Russia that, until then, were more remote from Moscow than was many a foreign country.

◇◇◇◇◇◇◇◇◇◇◇◇◇◇◇◇◇◇◇◇◇◇◇◇

From the mid-nineteenth century onwards, great railways began opening up the world's largest land masses. The sheer challenge of building Russia's Trans-Siberian Railway – the world's longest – represented the greatest feat of all, closely followed by the United States' Transcontinental line and the Canadian Pacific Railway. Although pioneering passengers also travelled these lines, they were designed primarily for freight – whether carrying construction and other goods to open up the interior or bringing raw materials from the hinterland to the industrial cities. In 1865 the far-sighted American George Pullman introduced his first sleeping car, the aptly named Pioneer. This suddenly opened up the possibility of reasonably civilised long-distance passenger rail travel across unruly badlands. Inspired by this, the Belgian entrepreneur Georges Nagelmackers founded the Compagnie Internationale des Wagons-Lits (CIWL) and created Europe's first luxury train, the famous Orient Express that began running from Paris to Constantinople (Istanbul) in 1883. The period from then until the outbreak of the Second World War – and especially following the hiatus of 1914–18 – qualifies as the 'golden age' of rail travel.

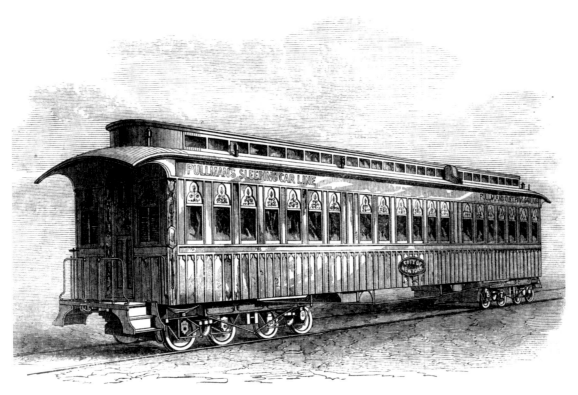

It should be emphasised that, golden or not, rail travel was by no means always luxurious or, for that matter, particularly fast. Much of the spell cast by such catchphrases derives from the romance of being able to travel long distances in comparative comfort through countries that in those days were scarcely touristed, if at all. Thanks to the train it was no longer necessary to rely on appalling roads in all weathers (with or without bandits), in cases of breakdown with no guarantee of finding better accommodation for the night than a barn or a haystack. There is no question that the aura of romance still clinging to trains like the Orient Express derives from its having been, for half a century, an adventure to travel on them. Modern period-costume films such as those of Agatha Christie's 1934 novel *Murder on the Orient Express* can somehow suggest a degree of luxury that was often lacking, even though the train being held up for days on end by snowdrifts was always a possibility in winter, as Agatha Christie had herself experienced.

British passengers would leave London on a train grandly called the Orient Express even though it was merely a first-class connection down to Dover, where either the Southern Railway's purpose-built ferry *Canterbury* (1929) or a French vessel took the passengers over to Calais where they re-embarked on a French CIWL train to Paris. There they made their way from the Gare du Nord to the Gare de Lyon, where they picked up the Simplon

His sleeping cars made George Pullman famous worldwide and, like many a successful industrialist, he founded a town for his employees. Not all were grateful: 'We are born in a Pullman house, fed from the Pullman shops, taught in the Pullman school, catechized in the Pullman Church, and when we die we shall go to the Pullman Hell.'

Orient Express. I know this because in August 1937 my mother travelled
on the Orient Express to visit her brother, who was working for the Anglo-
Iranian Oil Company (later BP) in Abadan on the Persian Gulf. Luckily for
the family she kept a journal, her vivid account still further fleshed out with
long letters home. 'Left Victoria 2 p.m. for Dover,' she began. 'Apart from
feeling terribly grand in a 1st Class Pullman, journey uneventful. French
boat – least necessary comfort – & there was a bit of a swell.' Once in Calais
she picked up the train to Paris where she changed stations and boarded
the Orient Express proper on which – as a woman in her twenties travelling
alone – she had a sleeping compartment to herself. When she woke at 5 a.m.
they were in Switzerland.

No doubt, on a long journey, part of the romance derives from unexpected
travelling companions who board the train at stations en route. On my
mother's trip, somewhere in northern Italy they picked up 'a charming
elderly Scotsman… who turned out to be Sir Malcolm Watson, head of the

The dining car of the Orient Express more as my mother would have known it.

Previous page: A poster for the route my mother took in 1937 to visit her brother in Abadan, Persia [Iran]. Like all such posters it manages to convey the romance of the exotic. There is no mention of having to cross the Syrian desert in battered cars.

London Institute of Tropical Hygiene who was off to inspect the medical side of a mine miles south of Beograd [Belgrade] which we reach tomorrow a.m.' In her same carriage was a tall, bronzed man. 'He's going to Baghdad – Government job – Gascoigne Hogg by name – so he & I will finish the journey together.' The Express stopped at large towns where the passengers wrote and posted postcards or went to the station bar for a drink. My mother commented on the lack of roads and motor vehicles throughout the Balkans, the beauty of the landscape, the Ruritanian police lounging on platforms and the 'shepherd girls and cow boys minding the beasts & peasants at work in the fields'. She was clearly fascinated by everything while drily noting the minor discomforts she and her fellow-travellers experienced as they left western Europe further behind. The coaches might still have been Pullman but the locomotives and their fuel could be from anywhere. 'Have just been through a fearful tunnel. What *do* they burn? It was like a gas attack, the fumes being sulphur dioxide. Soaked a hankie in water to make a gas mask as one simply couldn't breathe but got enough in me to make the lungs feel worried. Rather like mild asthma. We all coughed a lot.' As a qualified anaesthetist she was well able to identify the gas in the engine's smoke.

At Ankara she must either have swapped compartments or else the windows of the entire train were suddenly fitted with insect-proof screens.

'I like my new self-contained flat,' my mother observed whimsically, 'but the wire gauze window makes it feel like a meat safe. Still, it keeps livestock out & the flies have been troublesome. Midges don't scare but Turkish tobacco does! And this coal is better than the last lot: the smuts are nil compared with that.' Nor, in those pre-air conditioning days, were restaurant coaches quite the cool, relaxed gourmet experiences that films might suggest. 'As we lunched the temperature was 96°F in the dining room & G. H. said it felt more as it was damp. After lunch I retired to my T. E. Lawrence but before long the sweat trickled down so much it kept tickling so stripped & washed & was a bit cooler. I feel frightfully well – appetite like a horse – but then, after café au lait at 7 a.m. we get nil till 12.30 & then nothing till 7.30 p.m.'

The Orient Express ended in Istamboul (my mother's period spelling, as in Graham Greene's *Stamboul Train*). After that, her journey to Baghdad became rather tougher. She changed to the Taurus Express that, like the Orient Express, was also run by CIWL. The onward route was complex because it had to allow for difficult local terrain, awkward political agreements over frontiers, and even suitable supplies of wood or coal along the way to raise steam. They wove back and forth between Turkey and Syria. In eastern Turkey she noted: 'The women wear all sorts – sometimes clothes resembling the very poor European peasant or gypsy, some with their faces covered, some in baggy trousers. The woman is always covered – tho' her feet may be bare – yet I've seen women stripped to the waist.' Now once more in Syria, 'I hear we are "plus d'une heure et demi en retard". We left the restaurant car behind in Aleppo so no food or water & we are ravenous!'

The line headed back north-eastwards into Turkey until it reached Nusaybin on the Syrian border where it came to an abrupt end. From 1930 onwards, passengers had to disembark here and go by road to bridge a missing section of railway between Nusaybin and Kirkuk in Iraq, a distance of over 200 miles (322 km). At the Iraqi border they had to wait for hours in a stone room where the temperature was 106°F in the shade before setting off again in three 1927 Rolls-Royces with the luggage following behind in two Ford lorries – another 117 miles (188 km) of desert road to Mosul. 'What heat! It was terrific in the desert – just one long scorch – with a wind like a furnace. Nothing but yellow brown glare for miles & miles, with towers of yellow dust from the whirlwinds all over the place.' Eventually they reached Baghdad, where my mother was met and fêted by oil company representatives and was overjoyed to have a proper shower and to sleep in a bed that kept still. But her entire account shows she was

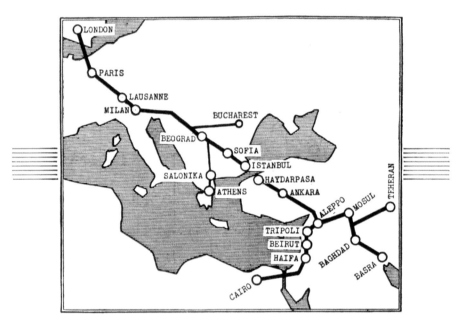

having the time of her life. She didn't much like Abadan itself, which was simply an unlovely and blistering oil town, but she and her brother made some trips inland and there was a constant round of swimming parties and dinners with the various expat wives and families. She even helped out in the local hospital, giving anaesthetics for operations. When it was time for her return journey she did not at all relish going back to 'boring England and dreary London' – a judgement her own son was later to inherit.

◇◇◇◇◇◇◇◇◇◇◇◇◇◇◇◇◇◇◇◇◇◇◇

It is easy to see why, despite having pioneered the railway, Britain never quite managed to make it the glamorous and even romantic form of travel it became elsewhere, when one could fall asleep in one country and wake to hear station porters speaking another language. It is simply a matter of geography. The distances between major British cities are just not great enough to make it worthwhile to run more than a handful of Pullman-style sleepers for a single night's journey. Furthermore, most rail networks' biggest earner by far was carrying freight, not passengers. However, first-class travel in daytime expresses could be made to pay if it was sufficiently uprated to be sold as luxury travel. This was nowhere more true than on the two main London to Scotland routes that were competitively served by rival companies: the London, Midland and Scottish Railway (LMS) which owned the west coast line to Glasgow; and the London North Eastern Railway (LNER) that monopolised the east coast line to Edinburgh. Of the so-called 'big four' rail companies that had been formed by the Railways Act of 1921, LMS was the largest and LNER the second-largest.

Each of the two claimed to be the better, and the rivalry between them was intense. This duel had been going on since the middle of the nineteenth century, when the various private rail companies that owned stretches of the two routes began seriously competing for custom. They did this by offering restaurant cars, plush upholstery and other appurtenances of Victorian and Edwardian stylish travel such as ladies-only and smoking carriages. Yet for decades there was an unwritten truce between the rivals that they would not compete for speed, mainly because pushing steam engines to their limit greatly increased coal consumption and the additional expense could wipe out any profit margin. The distance by rail on both mainline routes from London to Scotland was roughly 400 miles and generally took a leisurely eight and a quarter hours – an average speed of only 48 mph (77 kph) despite the trains being referred to as 'expresses'.

Opposite: In 1930 the ability to go by train from London to Basra or Cairo was perhaps less astonishing than being able to fly there. But it was still an adventure, one without airsickness and motor noise as well as being less likely to be delayed by bad weather or mechanical breakdown.

**ANT CARS
E·R**

The image that both
LNER and LMS wanted
to promote for their daily
expresses to Scotland
was one of sophisticated
comfort for the well-heeled.
The train companies were
just beginning to feel the
competition flying could
offer their busy executive
passengers.

By the late 1920s road vehicles had improved in speed and reliability and multiplied to such an extent that lorries, buses and cars began to threaten the railways' monopoly of long-distance travel and goods haulage. Feeling this pressure, in 1932 LMS and LNER agreed to suspend their gentlemen's pact and from then on the rivalry between the two companies was once more on a 'no holds barred' basis. It was clear to both that they needed some radically new engines, and not merely in order to compete in speed. They also badly needed a new image. This was now an age of expanding air travel and fast, luxury saloon cars. By comparison steam looked hopelessly old-fashioned, a throwback to the early nineteenth century with connotations of heavy engineering and industrial grime. Somehow this perception had to be revamped and the daily London to Scotland service made fast and luxurious enough to be a serious prospect for businesspeople hurrying to meetings, as well as chic enough for passengers who wanted to do the journey in style. The trouble was that 'style' meant trains of greatly increased weight, what with restaurant cars, onboard kitchens and chefs, wood-panelled compartments with heavily upholstered seats, and washrooms with plentiful water for the porcelain sinks and flushing lavatory bowls. This in turn demanded more powerful engines capable of hauling it all, and faster as well.

The competition became one between two exceptional engineers, both born in 1876. LNER's chief mechanical engineer was Nigel Gresley, who had designed the company's *Flying Scotsman* class engines in 1923. These undoubtedly gave LNER the edge in speed, being the first steam locomotives with a recorded speed of over 100 mph (161 kph) in passenger service. To combat this threat LMS headhunted William Stanier, who was chief mechanical engineer at Great Western Railway's Swindon works and had an equal reputation for brilliance. Although the two competing lines were more or less the same in length there was no doubt that LNER's east coast was the easier route, being more level and straighter. The west coast line had many twists and turns with speed limits on them, as well as hills. Above all there was the long haul up Shap Fell, which demanded a locomotive with unusual power.

At LNER, and conscious of the need for an up-to-date image, Nigel Gresley decided to embrace the trend that was equally apparent in the design of cars and aircraft – that of streamlining. His beautifully sculpted new A4 locomotive was the first of several examples in its class, its smoothly

Nigel Gresley, LNER's chief engineer, whose existing A3 *Flying Scotsman* locomotives gave his company an edge in speed over those of the rival LMS.

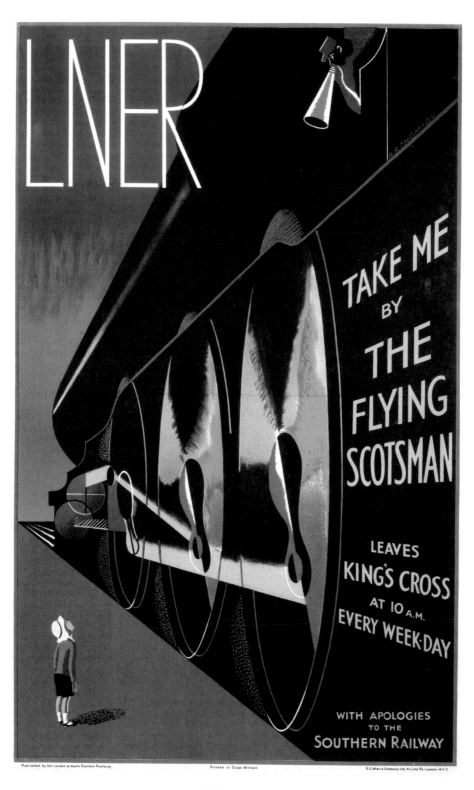

A 1932 LNER poster.

Capable as they were, these engines dated from 1923 and looked old-fashioned at a time when steam was everywhere else being overtaken by cars and aircraft and passengers wanted to be stylishly modern.

haunched design being most familiar today as that of the famous *Mallard*. Another was named in honour of the 1935 silver jubilee of King George V and Queen Mary. The entire train looked sensational, being streamlined from engine to guard's van as well as painted silver from end to end. On its first outing from London King's Cross to Grantham with the press on board, the *Silver Jubilee* not only wowed everyone who saw it streak past, but it broke four world records and twice attained 112.5 mph (181 kph). Once the type had begun the *Flying Scotsman*'s regular 10 a.m. scheduled run from King's Cross to Edinburgh, LNER could sell it as not only fast but true upmarket travel. There was an entire kitchen carriage with a proper chef in a white hat and correctly uniformed waiters to serve the meals. Advertising posters appeared showing a picture of a uniformed waiter with the tag word 'discretion' in capitals across it and an appended explanation: 'Discretion in mixing cocktails and serving crusted port – regard for our passengers' eupeptic welfare – these are qualities that distinguish the LNER waiter…' It all said quality for the Quality (who else would appreciate 'crusted' port and the understated use of 'discretion', let alone know what 'eupeptic' meant?).

From the start the new service was a success. At a stroke, Gresley had somehow managed to throw off the nineteenth-century associations of steam and rebrand LNER's express trains as a completely modern form of travel in the grand style, while stealing a march on their LMS rivals (even though Gresley

William Stanier worked as chief engineer at GWR before being head-hunted by LMS. It was there that he designed his Princess class *Coronation* engine that proved a real challenge for Gresley's A4s in both performance and looks.

Previous spread: *Stanier's beautifully streamlined 1937* Coronation *– a Duchess class loco he designed for LMS whose stunning modernist looks beguiled everyone, especially those who didn't know it was simply a sculpted shell bolted onto a magnificent but grimy coal-burning engine.*

later calculated that the streamlining on his A4 locos like *Mallard* probably added a maximum of 4 mph (6 kph) to their top speed, and very likely less).

Within a year William Stanier had hit back. In 1937 he and his design assistant, Tom Coleman, uprated their previous Princess Royal-class engine design and produced a new and very powerful locomotive that Coleman then insisted must be streamlined. This was *Coronation*, named for the newly crowned George VI. It was the first of several streamlined engines later to be known as the Duchess class and designed to pull the Coronation Scot service to Glasgow. Privately, Stanier shared his rival's scepticism about streamlining as an aid to better performance, probably because he understood the complexity of the air streams that caused drag under and between the carriages. However, he acknowledged that, marketing ploy or not, after LNER's success with streamlining LMS might have a severe image problem if it bucked the trend. Coleman's streamlining of the engine was even more radical than that of LNER. On *Coronation*'s first public outing from Euston to Crewe and back the press were particularly struck by how futuristic and graceful the beautiful blue-painted engine and tender looked, with a moustache of white go-faster stripes trailing from both sides of its beautifully rounded front.

Coronation's inaugural trip turned out to be a triumph but came dangerously close to being an appalling disaster. Nearing Crewe, and as the train drew closer to *Silver Jubilee*'s speed record of 112.5 mph (181 kph), the driver went for broke and gave the locomotive full throttle until they inched past LNER's record and broke it at 114 mph (183 kph). At that climactic moment the four people on the footplate realised with horror that Crewe was now barely a mile and a half away and despite emergency braking there was no way they were going to be able to stop smoothly in time. Worse, the station was built on a curve that had a maximum speed limit of 20 mph (32 kph). *Coronation* hit this while still travelling at 57 mph (92 kph) and barely stayed on the rails. As it was, the sudden heavy lurching alarmed the passengers and smashed a good deal of crockery in the dining coach until the train shuddered to a halt, brake shoes glowing. It is likely that only the men on the footplate realized just how close to catastrophe they had come. But by the time the train steamed back into Euston all was forgotten and all aboard were delighted to learn they had just been party to a new speed record. However, it was by no means a world speed record (at that point 10 mph faster at 124.5 mph [200 kph], held since the previous year by the German streamliner 05 002). It was merely another forceful step in the age-old rivalry with LNER, LMS now being able truthfully to claim theirs as the faster service between London and Scotland.

Stanier's powerful new locos represented a considerable triumph for their designer, hauling heavy coaches over 400 miles (644 km) nonstop in under six hours at an average of 70 mph (113 kph). All the same, the heads of the rival companies met discreetly once again and agreed a new truce on speed because at this rate it was obvious that sooner or later one or other of their expresses would come to grief, and a high-speed accident would be fatal to reputation as well as to passengers. Henceforth, the new emphasis was to provide still-better service and the fastest times as consistent with safety. Despite this, the old rivalry was evidently still alive and kicking and it was clearly a matter of pride to LNER that it should reclaim the speed record. This it famously did in 1938 when their five-months-old *Mallard* sailed past LMS's 114 mph (183 kph) and just managed to overtake the Germans' 124.5 mph (200 kph) when it briefly touched 126 mph (203 kph): a world record for a steam locomotive that stands to this day.

Not long after this, the Second World War put a stop to luxury travel everywhere. In Britain and elsewhere the streamlined shells were unbolted from the engines, the luxury coaches were shunted into sidings, and the younger chefs and waiters swapped their fancy company livery for military uniforms. Besides, despite the inspired efforts of engineers like Gresley and Stanier, it could no longer be disguised that steam really was old-fashioned and inefficient, at a time when the newest big American locomotives were diesel- or electric-powered and many lines in Europe (and even some in Britain) were already electrified.

At the time of writing in 2019 there came news that in the UK a new fleet of Caledonian sleeper trains had been unveiled. These are offering en-suite double rooms as well as upgraded ordinary sleeper carriages, each with six showers. Announcing this, a spokesman for the fleet began with the now-obligatory mantra, 'Safety is absolutely paramount for us', as though they had originally planned to run dangerous but thrillingly topless observation cars and had then thought better of it. 'But beyond that,' he went on, 'this is a hospitality experience. People are now very much looking for a decent experience – whether it is in a restaurant, a shop or indeed travelling on a

The first American 'streamlined' train was the Adams Windsplitter of 1900. The streamlining would have made no difference to its speed, but it was an important early visual token of modernity.

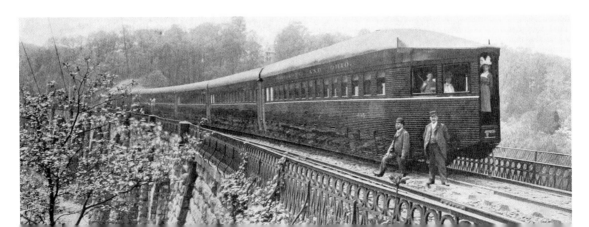

train – and we have gone after that market.'[2] His remarks are the perfect yardstick for measuring the true distance between the elegant interwar years of LNER's 'discretion', when trained waiters knew how to serve crusted port, and today, when people will pay premium prices for merely a 'decent hospitality experience', whatever that is.

◇◇◇◇◇◇◇◇◇◇◇◇◇◇◇◇◇◇◇◇◇◇◇◇

The idea of streamlining locomotives and their tenders – come to that, entire trains – was certainly not pioneered by Britain. A short, privately printed book on the subject was published in the United States as early as 1892: Frederick Upham Adams's *Atmospheric Resistance and its Relations to the Speed of Trains*. Little read at the time though it was, in 1900 the book convinced the Baltimore & Ohio Railroad's management to fit the first streamlining panels to the tender and carriages of a train, calling it the 'Adams Windsplitter'. It was soon calculated that they made almost no difference to the train's speed, probably because at the time so little was understood of the way drag forms. Yet the idea of giving locomotives as well as entire trains this cosmetic treatment increasingly caught on across America for the same reason that it was to in Britain and continental Europe – it lent what was an old technology the aura of modernity and speed.

If fast and elegant rail travel could be found anywhere between the wars, it was surely at its most developed in the United States. Immensely powerful locomotives were built to match the country's huge distances, its testing terrain and the rapidly advancing industrialization that demanded massive freight haulage. Some of these locomotives were giants with up to four pairs of driving wheels and putting out 170,000 horsepower. The swifter engines hauled passenger trains like Lehigh Valley Railroad's famous *Black Diamond Express* between New York and Buffalo, which ran from 1896 to 1959. In its day it was known as 'The Handsomest Train in the World' and 'The Honeymoon Express'. Its standards of first-class comfort can be judged by the fact that even in the late 1890s it had a 'Parlor Car' with a single row of well-upholstered armchairs on either side of the aisle, all set at an angle and offering passengers the illusion of being in their own sitting rooms.

Certainly when it came to streamlining, American locomotives led the world in sheer numbers and variety. Over the years some 1,800 were given streamlining facelifts. By the 1930s these tended to reflect the prevailing 'streamline moderne' look that had overtaken so much American industrial design. Underneath, of course, were the same muscular locomotives; but many of the streamlined designs that disguised them had only recently been made possible by the invention of a technique for shot-welding stainless steel to make aerodynamically smooth body shells (this was a crossover from the discovery of how to make aircraft fairings and domestic appliances like refrigerators with rounded corners). It was a technological breakthrough exploited by some of the most famous 1930s American industrial designers, including Otto Kuhler, Raymond Loewy, Donald Dohner, Henry Dreyfuss, Norman Bel Geddes and Buckminster Fuller. Together, they and their period produced a 'look' for machines and consumer products that is still clearly traceable today. Yet, where trains (and even cars) were concerned, although the 1930s fashion for streamlining had its roots in aerodynamics, it had virtually no practical effect on either economy or performance. The trains were so long that topping and tailing them with streamlined engines and observation cars offered no real advantage other than attracting publicity and passengers. In this, with their stylish modernity, they were highly effective.

What is generally reckoned as the first successful American streamliner was the Chicago, Burlington and Quincy Railroad's *Zephyr* of 1934. It billed itself as 'America's First Diesel Streamline Train' and in its first year it set a new speed record for a start-stop journey, averaging just short of 78 mph

Erie's massive 2-8-8-8-2 Triplex loco was one of several designs of US engines designed to haul prodigious loads. Built in 1914, the Triplex was never a success, using up most of its steam at speeds above 10 mph (16kph) and losing traction as it consumed coal and water.

The Pioneer *Zephyr* trainset built for the Burlington Route in 1934. The first diesel-engined streamliner, it could achieve speeds of well over 100 mph (161 kph). With its integrated cowcatcher, it looked like a plausible form of transport for a post-steam world.

(125.5 kph) for thirteen hours on the unbroken 1,000-mile journey between Denver and Chicago. On one section it touched 112.5 mph (181 kph). That same year New York Central's wonderful-looking streamliner *Commodore Vanderbilt* formed part of the company's 'Great Steel Fleet' whose stylish locos hauled fast, very luxurious passenger services over long distances. Typically, these trains would consist of an observation car, lounges, double bedrooms, roomettes, dining and buffet cars. This was seriously comfortable travel. The Pennsylvania Railroad had very similar, all-Pullman trains, the main difference being that their GG1 class locomotives were electric. In 1937 the New York, New Haven and Hartford Railroad commissioned Otto Kuhler to streamline its big I-5 class Hudsons to pull famous passenger trains like the *Yankee Clipper*. Both crews and passengers loved these trains for their speed and stylishness. Kuhler fulfilled his brief in an arresting style that culminated in 1938 with the beautiful engines that pulled the *Twentieth Century Limited*. The Pennsylvania Railroad's S1 of 1939, designed by Raymond Loewy, was so elegant it was exhibited at the New York World's Fair that same year.

With the exception of Europe's Orient Express, much of the stylish image of between-the-wars rail travel derives, via Hollywood, from American long-distance trains. Maybe the combination of wide-open spaces and relaxed, attentive service distils an atmosphere in which either drama or romance have the time and the space in which to develop – something that feels less common in European films of the period, probably because neither the trains nor the distances allowed for it to the same degree. Also, of course, in the 1930s with fascism in Spain and Italy and Nazism in Germany the issue of

C,B&Q's Blackhawk *Aeolus 4000* steam engine in 1937. It was basically a 4-6-4 loco with a stainless steel 'streamliner' shroud covering engine and tender. This added nothing to its speed on the Chicago – Denver run, but it looked terrific.

Above: In 1934, New York Central line created its *Commodore Vanderbilt* loco with a streamlined shell covering a Hudson 4-6-4 engine and named it after the railroad's founder.

Left: Penn Railroad's Class GG1 electric locos hauled the Congressional service from 1934 for many years. This early electrification of a line was a success, but the outlay was considerable and for years the system was better exploited over European shorter distances.

frontiers became increasingly obtrusive. There was never anything very romantic about knowing that the door of one's sleeping compartment might be wrenched open by an SS officer's gloved hand at four in the morning with a demand for one's papers.

◇◇◇◇◇◇◇◇◇◇◇◇◇◇◇◇◇◇◇◇◇◇◇◇

In the 1930s a positive rash of streamlined locomotives, and sometimes entire trains, also broke out in Europe. In Britain, apart from Stanier's Duchess class and Gresley's A4s, the Great Western Railway tried streamlining their King class loco *King Henry VII* by sticking a nose-cone on the front. This did virtually nothing to improve the engine's speed and even less to improve its looks; it was simply a feeble nod towards fashion. In France the Paris, Lyon and Mediterranean Railway (PLM) produced a handsomely streamlined version of one of their Atlantic class locos, the 221B. The Czech SD produced its 386

One of Milwaukee Road's
Hiawathas. Their Class
A 4-4-2 steam locos
shrouded in Art Deco
streamlining, the trains
were in direct competition
with the Burlington
Route's Zephyrs. They
were cannily advertised
as being 'Ahead of the
Times'.

series from the mid-1930s and the Polish Pm36-1 had a smart aerodynamic fairing with 'haunches' not unlike those of Gresley's *Mallard*.

Germany was also streamlining its trains. An early example showed a direct crossover from aviation: the Schienenzeppelin ('rail Zeppelin') of 1929. This was the work of Franz Kruckenberg, who had designed aircraft in the First World War. It was a dirigible-shaped railcar somewhat alarmingly driven by a big unprotected twin-bladed airscrew at the back. It could seat forty passengers and could reach an astonishing maximum speed of 143 mph (230 kph). In 1931 this became the new world rail speed record and it lasted until 1954, although it still stands as the record for a petrol-powered railcar. Kruckenberg's design combined light weight with aerodynamic streamlining, an essential combination in today's ultra-fast expresses and bullet trains. Much less essential in any modern design is a large propeller whirring at the train's rear. Further Zeppelin influence was to be seen in the United States, where in 1935 the New York, New Haven and Hartford Railroad introduced the Comet, a product of the Goodyear-Zeppelin Company.

From 1933 Germany's new Nazi government was anxious to showcase its industry and engineering. That year saw the *Fliegender Hamburger* (the 'Hamburg Flyer') enter service between Berlin and Hamburg. It was a fast diesel train essentially consisting of the engine and driver's cab pulling a

From 1937 Crusaders ran from Philadelphia to Jersey City and comprised two stainless steel coaches, two observation cars and a 'tavern-dining' car. From 1950 they were pulled – as here – by General Motors FP7 diesel-electric locos.

Right: One of Union Pacific's experimental steam turbine/electric locos of 1939. Although immensely powerful and reputed to be capable of 125 mph (201 kph), they proved mechanically unreliable and saw little service.

Below: In France a streamlined shell was fitted over the retired Class 221A Atlantics in 1937 to produce the 221B. This gave PLM's Paris – Lyon service the sleek new look of modernity.

Above: The Czech 386. Another striking pre-1939 effort to make an old steam engine look up to date. Sheer beef in greyhound's clothing.

Poland's Pm36-1 was one of two prototypes dating from 1936. The following year it went on to win a Gold Medal at the Paris International Exposition of Art and Technology. After 1939 it was absorbed into Hitler's Reichsbahn and didn't survive the war.

single carriage – again, more of a railcar than a conventional train. But it was capable of 99 mph (159 kph) and was the product of serious wind-tunnel research to aid its streamlining. This maybe added impetus to Deutsche Reichsbahn's three 05 class streamlined steam locomotives that entered service between 1935 and 1937. In 1935 one broke the world's speed record for steam locomotives at 119.1 mph (191.7 kph) and the following year broke it again with a 124.5 mph (200.4 kph) run. It was perhaps not aesthetically very pleasing even if its streamlining was aerodynamically determined. Rather, it was severely – even brutally – functional, which of course has its own beauty. But no one could deny that these three locomotives were fast and hauled prestige trains that were very much a part of a golden railway age. Indeed, had one of them raced against *Mallard* it is by no means certain that the British engine would still hold the absolute world record for steam, because its bare 1.5 mph (2.4 kph) edge may have been more than accounted for by the slightly downhill track on which it was achieved. We will never know.

In 1935 the Goodyear-Zeppelin Company built the Comet streamliner. It had three cars and was double-ended so didn't need to be turned around at a terminus. The exterior was machined aluminium with dark blue stripes.

Above: Union Pacific's M-10000 City of Salina: the US's first internal combustion-powered streamliner that paved the way for the big diesel locos that soon followed.

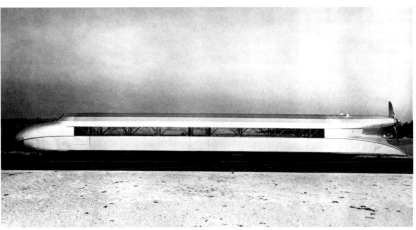

With its aircraft engine the ultra-fast Schienenzeppelin of 1929 owed clear debts to aviation. The huge airscrew at the rear must surely have worried nervous passengers waiting on platforms. The German army eventually broke it up for parts in 1939.

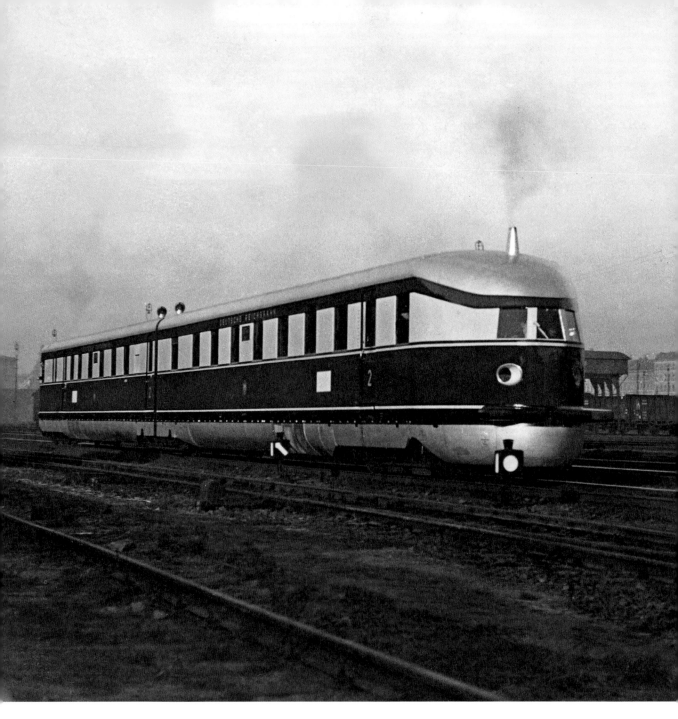

For a while the 'Hamburg Flyer' diesel-electric trainset of 1933 ran the world's fastest scheduled rail service. Amazingly, it survived the war and was back on its old run in 1957.

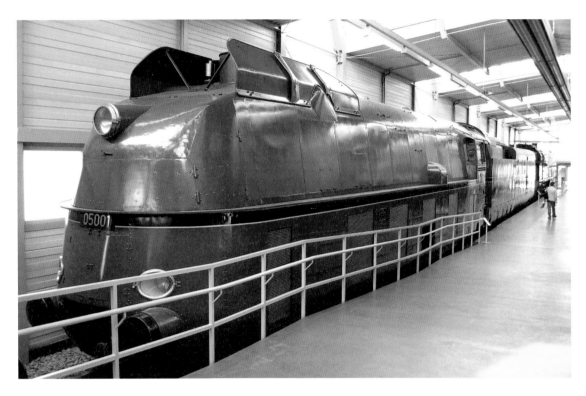

Above: The first of three Class 05 streamlined locos built for the German railway dates from 1935. All three were back in regular service from 1951–58 but only No. 05001 survives to this day in the Verkehrsmuseum in Nurenberg.

Right: An Italian ETR 200 streamliner from 1937 still looks amazingly modern, unlike many of its more extravagantly styled contemporaries of various nationalities. The basic type survived until 1993; surely a tribute to its far-sighted design.

Previous spread: *General Motors' Aerotrain was introduced in the mid-1950s and its styling shows an unmistakable crossover from GM's Automotive division. It was designed by the 28-year-old Chuck Jordan, who became Cadillac's chief designer at the height of the craze for fins.*

Mussolini's Italy was equally keen to show that it, too, was competitive on rails. In 1937 it introduced the electric ETR 200 class streamliners. These consisted of three carriages with a wind-tunnel-designed driving car that would still look quite modern today. The first of these soon achieved 125 mph (201 kph) and in 1939 an ETR 212 achieved 126 mph (203 kph) on the Milan–Florence run. By the outbreak of war these trains on the Bologna–Rome–Naples run were considered the most comfortable, the quietest and the cleanest of all European express trains. Overhead electrification with the use of pantographs on the locomotive's roof was shown as definitely the way forward. The days of smoke and smuts, of dusty coal heaps and water cranes for refilling engines at the platform's end, were numbered.

◇◇◇◇◇◇◇◇◇◇◇◇◇◇◇◇◇◇◇◇◇◇◇◇

If any trains in the first half of the twentieth century qualify for the accolade of being fast, beautiful and luxurious, they are most likely to be those of the 1930s United States. It was there that the most advanced materials and engineering techniques were combined with the demands of geography to produce maximum speed and comfort over long journeys. Even at this stylish peak, however, the private railways could see the inroads on their passenger custom being made by aircraft like Douglas's new DC-3 and its DST sleeper version. The level of comfort might not yet have been the same, but many more miles could be covered in a three-hour flight than by the fastest express train, and in the absence of gourmet meals more cheaply. Increasingly, most railroad companies would concentrate more on hauling freight than on passenger services.

This pattern was to continue after 1945 until today's position throughout much of the world was reached, when most long-distance journeys are made by air. On the railways today there is sometimes little on offer between cattle-truck conditions for local commuters and expensive, elderly tourist-style journeys on scenic routes such as through the Canadian Rockies or across Australia and the United States. However, with today's 'bullet' trains and the rakishly streamlined ultra-high-speed trains in Japan and China and even in Europe, this trend may perhaps be reversed before long. Much depends on whether a fashion for virtuous, 'green' travel takes hold with people abandoning with relief the ever-grimmer experience of flying. This probably is the way by which the train could make a comeback and even regain a 'Concorde' social status for its classy speed and elegance. If so, it will no doubt be reflected by the fares.

Meanwhile, the old between-the-wars allure of fast, stylish rail travel on long romantic journeys scarcely any longer exists (as anyone might suspect who has travelled on an overnight sleeper from Cairo to Luxor). Even the Trans-Siberian Railway's romance has been dimmed by backpackers. But the unspoiled places of the world, where tourists taking half-witted selfies can't be found, are a rapidly shrinking resource. Those of us who did our youthful travelling in a far less tamed and uniform world can count ourselves truly lucky. A major part of the 'golden age' of travel was its utter lack of speed and elegance. What it offered was the romance of self-sufficiency; the excitement of being out of touch with home for weeks or even months at a stretch. There were only irregular postcards, out-of-date letters randomly collected *poste restante* from various flyblown post offices, and in extremis desperate telegrams and cables dispatched from frontier towns. The whole point was the freedom: to go adventuring in a world where no one – often including you – knew where you were; when all communication was with strangers, face-to-face in motley languages, as it always was throughout human history until these last few lethal decades.

Next spread: Capable of speeds up to 177 mph (285 kph), the Japanese 700 series Shinkansen bullet trains show the phenomenon of hi-tech convergent evolution. Today, such high-speed trains have a tendency to resemble each other closely, for severe aerodynamic and mechanical reasons.

AFTERWORD
Stylishness

People today still view with a kind of envious nostalgia the aura surrounding various modes of travel that burgeoned between 1900 and 1945 – well before most of the admirers or even their parents were born. The images that feed this nostalgia come via books like this one, from newsreel footage, from old magazine illustrations, from novels and films, and above all from Hollywood.

Despite – or maybe because of – the savagery of the First World War, an Edwardian idea of stylishness persisted in the 1920s to be wedded to the great technological advances the war had itself brought about. The result was a glamorous new world of speed and travel that for the most part still withheld (even as it promised) any real democratisation. It seemed to promise limitless horizons for everybody, even as the actual cost of accessing that world put it well beyond most people's means – capitalism's siren call, in short. Despite the countless third-class and steerage passengers down in the bowels of the great transatlantic liners; despite the 15 million Ford Model Ts chugging along dusty roads worldwide; and notwithstanding the millions of commuter miles daily clocked up by office drudges on interwar suburban railways, the notion persists that the interwar era was marked by a stylishness that today has been irrevocably lost.

The most obvious form of this stylishness was that of the better brands of car, if only because they were the most visible on a daily basis. In those interwar years the difference between upmarket and utility was nearly always glaring. Not until the early 1930s – and then only in America – did car manufacturers make any real effort to style their mass-produced vehicles by employing proper designers. As already noted, General Motors took the initiative, but only so that people could more easily judge from seeing one of its cars what rung of the economic ladder the driver occupied.

In many respects, today's various car categories have changed little from those of the 1930s, even as the technology has improved immeasurably. There are still utility runabouts (Honda Civics); solid family saloons (Volvos); sports cars for boy racers, footballers and balding bankers (Porsches and Ferraris); and hypercars for hyper-rich sheikhs (Bugatti Veyrons). As before, there is still practically no limit to how much one can spend on a car. As ever there is glitz and swank, over- and understated luxury. Yet the one thing that seems missing today when compared to the greatest cars of the 1920s and 1930s is *stylishness*: an elusive quality with a provocative trace of snobbery. In this supposedly egalitarian age it is as if no car is purposely designed to be stylish. Manufacturers may well hope their cars make a statement about a driver's bank balance, concern for safety or even 'green' credentials; but nobody appears to think purely in terms of style.

One reason for this is surely because any remaining novelty and mystique that motor vehicles once held vanished with the Second World War – to the point where these days they are widely viewed more as a regrettable menace. There is a great deal more money around now than there was ninety years ago and far more widely spread, and in much of the globe car ownership has long become no more than a commonplace necessity. It is hard to imagine any marque of contemporary automobile being described as 'stylish', no matter how expensive, since that is an epithet associated with a more leisured way of life back in the days when social exclusivities were better marked.

A graceless hunk of machinery, the Rolls-Royce Cullinan has abandoned all pretence of stylishness in favour of the tank-like 'school bully' look. The famous 'Spirit of Ecstasy' now seems quite lost without a radiator to stand on. The poor creature is apparently spring-loaded and can be felled from any angle.

The Cadillac Escalade. Just another SUV with smoked windows. The elegant flamboyance that once made Cadillacs so visually splendid is a thing of the past. The name inexplicably refers to medieval warfare: scaling ramparts with ladders, probably to be met by a shower of boiling tar.

The formerly great car marques faithfully reflect this absence. Today's latest Rolls-Royces and Cadillacs can sometimes share a vaguely similar 'look' in accordance with evolving fashion, as do the Sultan of Brunei's six specially ordered Bentley Dominators. Their genre could perhaps be called Dictators' Utility Vehicles. In a DUV all pretence of style and even of gracefulness has vanished. With their modishly boxy shape and slab-like fronts they somewhat resemble tanks or maybe bulldozers, presumably for shouldering their way imperiously onward, possibly through a road block or over a pitchfork-wielding *canaille*. In its present context of Rolls-Royce's hideously ugly SUV Cullinan, the once classically restrained and dignified Parthenon radiator grille now manages to hint at a disdainful snarl, while the Cadillac Escalade's own grille has widened into a greedy maw. No doubt these vehicles are designed to reflect a modern age beset with panic about personal security that did not preoccupy the designers of limousines a hundred years ago. At their best, those masterpieces exuded an effortless superiority; those of today a hi-tech belligerence. They may not be, but they look like vehicles whose passengers' relative importance is measured by the thickness of bulletproof glass, the reinforcing of floors against possible landmines and the ability to speed away over any terrain with all four tyres shot to ribbons. Above all, they no longer suggest royalty or Hollywood stars, and least of all gracious living.

A further bar to stylishness in many modern cars, especially in expensive sports models, is that their road-hugging lowness – so essential for road-holding performance – makes them almost impossible to get in or out of with anything approaching elegance. This is above all true for women, especially those with fashionably short skirts. This was long foreseen, to the extent that between the wars Swiss and French finishing schools were already offering instruction on how a lady could get in and out of a car elegantly, let alone decently. These days, a celeb's flash of underwear (or worse) might play well in the tabloids, but it is the very opposite of stylish.

◇◇◇◇◇◇◇◇◇◇◇◇◇◇◇◇◇◇◇◇◇◇◇◇◇◇

Today's comparative uniformity of style in nearly all cars (and 'bullet' trains and aircraft, come to that) has everything to do with the phenomenon of 'convergent evolution'. Until the Second World War, cars – and particularly aircraft – were still new enough as rapidly improving mechanical phenomena to reflect a degree of experimentation, both mechanically and stylistically. Different companies produced models that were often readily identifiable as being from that firm. An entire car could suggest its company – like any one of the magnificent between-the-wars models produced by the French ex-aircraft company Avions Voisin. Other cars might be recognisable from a characteristic bonnet mascot, Daimler's crinkled radiator top or Vauxhall's distinctive scalloped vee of flutes from the radiator back along both upper sides of the bonnet. This was often equally true of aircraft, as in Geoffrey de Havilland's instantly identifiable tail fins on his Moth series, or in the American Granville brothers' tubby Gee Bee racing aircraft that faithfully followed the 1930s 'streamline moderne' craze for teardrop-based aerodynamics.

A de Havilland DH 82 Tiger Moth with its instantly recognisable tail fin. Nearly all the Moth series and other de Havilland marques up to the Dragon Rapide retained this characteristic and elegant shape.

In other respects a car's distinction might once have stemmed from a more-or-less standard chassis being turned into a 'one-off', customers ordering their bodywork from a particular designer or coachbuilder. This might be quirky or extravagant, not to mention in dubious taste. The celebrated between-the-wars French coachbuilder Jean-Henri Labourdette took one customer's 1939 Rolls-Royce Phantom III and in 1947 produced a trademark Labourdette Vutotal body for it that, with its brass stripes and gold-plating, looks nothing like any ordinary Rolls-Royce. It is unquestionably individual and a one-off, if scarcely to everybody's taste. True, like Henry Ford with his Model T, most of today's car manufacturers will offer a basic model of a type plus a wide range of add-on extras and colours so that the buyer can 'personalise' it at whim. But the overall shape remains the same even as the rest tends to become poncier rather than more stylish – one of consumerism's indelible hallmarks.

Until 1939 gifted engineers were often given their head in order to introduce a particular mechanical innovation like a sleeve-valve engine or independent suspension, while coachbuilders were equally happy to experiment with fads such as boat tails or rumble seats. Yet, despite Ford's Model T, the Baby Austin and Douglas's DC-3, both motoring and flying remained largely beyond most people's means, and independent car makers, other than the big mass-producers on both sides of the Atlantic, went steadily out of business in the Depression following the Wall Street Crash of 1929. With them went a good deal of the individuality and extravagance of design that countless small firms had offered.

The Gee Bee Model R Super Sportster was built for an air race in 1932 which it easily won. Its aerodynamics were designed for fast turns and were effective but dangerous, and several Gee Bees proved fatal to their pilots. This is a modern replica.

J-H Labourdette's 1947 Vutotal body for a Rolls-Royce Phantom III. Wonderfully gross in its way, it did at least continue the pre-war tradition of coachbuilders taking a manufacturer's complete chassis and engine and designing a body to suit a customer's individualism.

Only once the post-1945 economies in North America and Europe had improved enough to make car ownership increasingly widespread (and after the 1960s in Europe, air travel as well) did car and commercial aircraft companies become ever more dominated by standardisation. This was less apparent in military aircraft companies because the new technology of jet propulsion being developed (at vast public expense) beneath the spur of the Cold War allowed for some wild experimentation, especially in the United States. But where cars were concerned, unifying motives included the urge for economies of scale when building for mass markets as well as for economies of performance. This last criterion became particularly urgent following the global oil crisis triggered by OPEC in 1973 that led to the swift quadrupling of the cost of petrol. In addition, there were the economics of marketing and design in maintaining a car's fashionable 'look'.

This was convergent evolution; and the phenomenon is as apparent in commercial aircraft as it is in cars. These days most people couldn't tell an Airbus from a Boeing on sight, or either from a Chinese Comac C919, a Russian MC-21 or an Embraer E-Jet E2. With their uniformly swept-back wings and podded engines they all look pretty much the same to the untutored eye, apart from their airlines' livery. This is because they are all the result of tightly competitive physics: the same highly refined criteria in advanced aerodynamics and engine technology employed for marginal economic advantage. Furthermore, in an industry where profit margins are cut to the bone, the way the airlines arrange their seating means that for an overwhelming number of passengers any chance of glamour and style has been reduced to zero. People may understandably be envious of first-class passengers, but even they cannot pretend it is a stylish way to travel – the formulaic luxe is simply much less grim than cattle class.

When they announce a new type, aircraft manufacturers often produce advertising that tries to summon up the ghost of an old-fashioned stylishness. Thus, when Airbus introduced the new A380 in 2006, the publicity featured pictures of liner-style spaciousness with gyms, bars, sleeper cabins, lounges and staircases connecting the two floors. However, most of the images were computer-generated in an empty aircraft to show what *might* be done with so much space. The airlines had very different, more hard-headed ideas of what to do with it, and once they got their hands on the aircraft the vision of gyms and gracious dining became mirages, swamped by their specifications for the cost-effective realities of 'bums on seats' and carbon footprints per passenger mile.

Even in car design, aerodynamics have long played a role in styling (and critically so in today's Formula race cars). But now in the everyday commercial sector and with the primacy of fuel thriftiness, they assume a new importance. These days the concept of 'streamlining' sounds wonderfully old-fashioned in a world where the phrase 'spare tyre' is already acquiring a ring almost as archaic as that of 'running board' or 'starting handle'. Nevertheless, convergent evolution is playing its part here, too; and since much the same physical and evolutionary laws govern all these factors cars, like commercial airliners, have for years been looking much the same, most mass-market brands being practically indistinguishable to the casual eye and the majority of those pretty hideous at that. Above all, they are not stylish.

Today there are even more people conspicuously rich enough to order 'personalised' versions of expensive cars than there were in the 1920s and 1930s, although most seem to specify predictable things like getting their hypercar gold-plated or having the seats upholstered with panda fur.

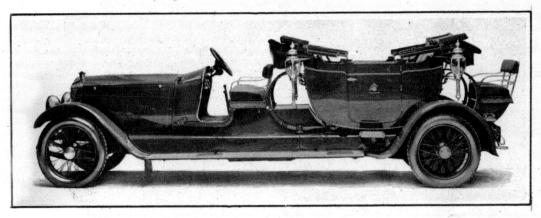

A STATE CAR—IN THE LIKENESS OF AN OLD COACH—BUILT FOR H.H. THE MAHARAJAH OF ALWAR : THE 40-H.P. LANCHESTER AS AN OPEN VEHICLE FOR CEREMONIAL OCCASIONS.

SPECIALLY BUILT FOR H.H. THE MAHARAJAH OF ALWAR : A 40-H.P. LANCHESTER STATE CAR—AS A CLOSED VEHICLE.
This interesting 40-h.p. Lanchester has been built for H.H. the Maharajah of Alwar, and is a State car, with a body on the lines of the State coaches used by royalty in this country.

The original 1919 40-horsepower Lanchester was reckoned the equal of a Rolls-Royce in terms of engineering quality, which was presumably why a maharajah chose it for this particular weird extravagance. Interesting that so many state and royal coaches still exist, defiantly unmodern.

The more outré one's taste, the more cachet one can accrue by flaunting it – standard human vulgarity, in short. Until 1939, India's numerous maharajahs ordered all sorts of money-no-object cars – mostly but by no means exclusively customised Rolls-Royces. In 1919 the Maharajah of Alwar bought a 40-horsepower Lanchester that had created a sensation at that year's London Motor Show where it cost more than one of Rolls-Royce's new but ageing Silver Ghosts. He ordered its chassis lengthened so the back part could accommodate a replica of a horse-drawn European coronation coach. It had raised seats at the rear for two footmen and sundry gold trimmings. The present-day counterpart of this preposterous vehicle is the Sultan of Brunei's ceremonial Rolls-Royce Silver Spur that has a sort of cloth-of-gold-covered gazebo at the back. The vehicle is further encrusted with 'an undisclosed amount of 24-carat gold' and the whole monstrosity is allegedly worth almost $15 million, though presumably only if it is melted down.

It is interesting that even as various decadent maharajahs were ordering their extravagant conveyances, European dictators with serious territorial conquest in mind were also taking delivery of their own bespoke parade cars. These were open tourers with plenty of room for standing in the back to salute cheering crowds. In the case of Mussolini, they were Alfa Romeo 6Cs, whereas Hitler's were Mercedes-Benz 770K 'great open touring cars' with bulletproof glass, armoured floor and sides and a panel at the back that could be quickly raised as a shield, as in James Bond's DB5. Although these German monsters weighed over five tons they could still manage a top speed of 112 mph (180 kph) and dictators worldwide would have had one on their shopping lists in preference to something merely regal. Like the big Alfa Romeos, they were strictly practical vehicles incorporating the very latest technology and neither car could be described as in any way gaudy. They were also too severely functional to be truly stylish.

Not a 'My Big Fat Gypsy Wedding' but the Sultan of Brunei's big fat wedding, for which he had one of his many Rolls-Royce Silver Spurs stretched and gold-plated. With the palanquin at the back, it is a sort of over-the-top version of the Maharajah of Alwar's Lanchester.

One of Sir Bernard and Lady Docker's post-war Daimlers, the DE 36 'Green Goddess' of 1948 – the most expensive car at that year's Motor Show. Mocking the Dockers is easy, but their car unquestionably recalled a pre-war stylishness while offering technical innovations like a speedometer that was switchable from mph to kph.

Occasionally, lavishly eye-catching cars could be thinly disguised self-advertising for commercial purposes. As noted earlier, in 1950 the British royals finally deserted British Daimlers – hitherto their preferred marque – in favour of Rolls-Royce. After the war, Daimler had fallen on hard times and the company's notorious chairman Sir Bernard Docker and his flashy second wife Norah set about raising its image by designing several show models, including ones complete with gold plating, gold stars, ivory dashboards and zebra-skin upholstery (mink being too hot to sit on, as Norah kindly explained to a dazzled newspaper hack). The so-called 'Green Goddess', a Hooper-bodied fast Daimler limo, unquestionably revived something of a pre-war stylishness. Lady Docker drove such glitzy cars around grey, impoverished, post-war London, revelling in the scandalised publicity they aroused in the popular press. The venture did little to revive Daimler's fortunes but everything to keep the Dockers in the limelight. Jesus Christ noted that we have the poor always with us; but it is just as true that we also have the rich, who often have deplorable taste, which is amusing and gives the rest of us a welcome excuse to scoff.

◇◇◇◇◇◇◇◇◇◇◇◇◇◇◇◇◇◇◇◇◇◇◇◇

It was the big passenger liners that had the necessary size to enable the shipping companies to set-dress their first-class spaces and display changing tastes in stylishness. By the time of the big Cunarders the most dramatic of these spaces, other than the inevitable chandeliered atrium and sweeping Hollywood-style staircase, were generally the dining rooms, which could often be extravagant to the point of absurdity. It is not quite clear what ambience they were supposed to suggest. *Aquitania*'s Pallas-Salon of 1913 was like a grand country house sitting room, complete with Corinthian pillars flanking a fireplace (with burning logs), plasterwork with murals, skylight windows, heavy armchairs and a sofa that seemed to reflect a vaguely art nouveau taste. What exactly was this grand luxe supposed to resemble? A very expensive hotel? A London club? The *Lusitania* and *Mauretania* both had lifts to take first-class passengers between floors (one uses the word advisedly in place of 'decks' since so much effort was expended on making the passengers forget they were at sea). The lifts' ironwork, the flanking carpeted staircase and the pillars here seem to suggest an upmarket Edwardian department store, a sort of oceangoing Derry & Toms.

For a century and a half now, some version of grand-luxe interior design and decor in passenger ships has become the norm. The underlying motive seems always to have been to make passengers forget that they were floating atop miles of cold dark brine and cocooned in a luxurious mobile hotel. Its apotheosis is the '5-star hotel experience' style favoured by modern cruise ships, which today opt less for Trump Tower baroque as their default design although some, such as Dreamlines, still seem to prefer the red-plush-and-chandeliers look.

As noted in an earlier chapter, almost from the beginning – and certainly from the 'booze cruises' of the Prohibition era – cruise ships have been increasingly designed to do everything possible to distract passengers from being aware of the sea as literally supporting the entire enterprise. As ever, stops are made at well-known tourist ports where, in the limited time available, passengers are presented with various 'experiences'. (Often just lunch and a visit to the local market. It's all about retail.) Everything seems designed to insert a painless wedge between the passengers and their wider environment. These days it is hard not to see this as mirroring the effect of social media, where people's attention is often near-monopolised by handheld devices and the world is seen literally at arm's length through the lens of their mobile phone. Virtual reality will presumably complete this isolation. If this is part of a trend in the design of modern cruise liners it seems oddly dated or misplaced in the context of increased awareness of global warming, the fragility of the natural world, the worsening condition of the sea, and so forth.

Look for instance at MSC's new (2019) *Bellissima*. Built at Saint-Nazaire, it is 315 metres (1,033 ft) long, 65 metres (213 ft) high, with nineteen decks, and cost £1 billion. It looks like a floating housing estate with a tuft of raked exhausts of various sizes emerging like quills from its back. Its capacity is for 5,686 passengers and 1,500 crew – a far cry from interwar cruises when 200 to 300 passengers were looked after by 800 crew as well as by their own servants. *Bellissima* contains a 100-yard-long 'promenade' of shops, a bowling alley, a Formula 1 simulator, twelve different restaurants, twenty bars with twenty varieties of champagne on offer, a water park on the topmost deck, a full-sized theatre for shows and seven children's playrooms. There are six 'elegant Swarovski staircases' on board, each step of which is set with 640 'Swarovski crystals'. There is also a Carousel Lounge that looks utterly hideous and would make a good picture contrast with the calm restraint of its counterparts in the elegant liners of yesteryear. As of 1 March 2019, *Bellissima* is selling eight nights 'around the Med' for £699 as a starting price. Other cruise ships launching in 2019 have go-kart tracks, rollercoasters and 'bumper cars' – presumably dodgems.

◇◇◇◇◇◇◇◇◇◇◇◇◇◇◇◇◇◇◇◇◇◇◇◇

The stylishness we have lost was inevitably associated with a degree of unashamed exclusivity, allied to a certain novelty. Although shameless extreme wealth exists today to a greater degree than ever before, the public's familiarity with its typical toys – the gold Rolls-Royces, private jets with saunas and oligarchs' liner-sized yachts – merely places them at the top end of consumerism. And consumerism is fatal to the stylish.

NOTES

INTRODUCTION
[1] Marozzi, Justin on Nan Shepherd's *The Living Mountain*, in *Slightly Foxed* 60, Winter 2018
[2] Quoted in Corn, Joseph J. and Horrigan, Brian: *Yesterday's Tomorrows* (Johns Hopkins University Press 1996), p. 94
[3] Peter Whigham (trans.), Catullus 4, *The Poems of Catullus* (Penguin, 1966), p. 53
[4] Quoted in: Parissien: *The Life of the Automobile* (Atlantic Books, 2013), opening of Chapter 4

SHIPS
[1] Quoted in Frame, Chris and Cross, Rachelle: *The Evolution of the Transatlantic Liner* (The History Press, 2013), p. 20
[2] Waterton, W. A.: *The Quick and the Dead* (Frederick Muller, 1956), p. 232

PLANES
[1] Quoted in Botting, Douglas: *Dr Eckener's Dream Machine* (HarperCollins, 2002), p.113
[2] Ibid. p. 116
[3] Ibid. p. 153
[4] Ibid. p. 233
[5] Ibid. p. 236

CARS
[1] From a Calkins & Holden campaign for Pierce-Arrow in 1915 quoted in Meikle, Jeffrey L.: *Twentieth Century Limited* (Temple University Press), p. 11
[2] Charteris, Leslie: *The Avenging Saint* (Pan, 1949), pp. 70 & 169
[3] See https://www.jewishvirtuallibrary.org/general-motors-and-the-third-reich
[4] Quoted in Kimes, B. R. ed., 'Bugatti' in *The Classic Car* (Classic Car Club of America, 1990), p. 632
[5] Quoted in Meikle, *op. cit.*, p. 144

TRAINS
[1] Ruskin, John: 'Carriages of Damned Souls' (*Globe*, 3 March 1887, p. 2)
[2] Ryan Flaherty, Caledonian Sleeper's managing director, quoted by BBC News 11 April 2019

IMAGE CREDITS

AKG

pp. 8–9, p. 12, p. 20, p. 27 (top), p .40, p. 53, pp. 66–7, p. 78, p. 84 (bottom), p. 113, p. 125, pp. 126–7, p. 135, p. 139 (bottom), p. 150 (bottom), p. 159, p. 160, p. 161, p. 163, pp. 168–9, p.187

Alamy

p. 4, p. 23, p. 25, p. 31 (top), p. 32, pp. 106–7, p. 111, p. 117, p. 122, p. 123, p. 124, p. 128, p. 130, p. 133 (top), p. 137 (bottom), p. 138 (top), p. 150 (top), p. 184, p. 185 (bottom), p. 189 (bottom), p. 190, p. 202, p. 205

Bridgeman

p. 157

Getty Images

p. 6, p. 11, p. 13, p. 14 (top), p. 26, p. 31 (bottom), p. 35, p. 43, p. 44, p. 45, p. 50, p. 55, p. 61, pp. 62–3, p. 76 (bottom), p. 80, p. 81, p. 95, p. 97, p. 98, p. 99, pp. 100–101, p. 102, p. 104, p. 105, pp. 108–9, p. 114, p. 120, p. 134, p. 136, p. 137 (top), p. 138 (bottom), p. 139 (top), pp. 140–141, pp. 142–3, pp. 144–5, p. 146 (top), p. 146 (bottom), p. 148, p. 149, p. 153, pp. 154–5, p. 164, p. 170, p. 171, pp. 172–3, p. 174, p. 175, pp. 176–7, p. 181, pp. 182–3, p. 186 (top), p. 186 (bottom), p. 191 (bottom), p. 192, pp. 194–5, pp. 198–9, p. 201, p. 210, p. 209, p. 213

Getty Images colourized by Marina Amaral

pp. 108–9

Mary Evans

p. 10, p. 27 (bottom), p. 33, p. 39, p. 46 (bottom), p. 47, p. 57, p. 58 (top), p. 58 (bottom), p. 59, p. 64, p. 70, p. 71, pp. 72–3, p. 74, p. 76 (top), p. 79 (top), p. 79 (bottom), p. 82, p. 84 (top), pp. 92–3, p. 151 (top), p. 162, p. 166, p. 185 (top), p. 188 (top), p. 204, p. 208

Wikimedia Commons

p. 14 (bottom), p. 15 (top), p. 15 (bottom), pp. 16–17, p. 18, p. 46 (top), p. 86, p. 87, p. 103, p. 119, p. 131 (top), p. 131 (bottom), p. 133 (bottom), p. 151 (bottom), p. 179, p. 188 (bottom), p. 193 (top), p. 193 (bottom), p. 206

Alon Siton / Historical Railway Images

p. 189 (top), p. 191 (top)

INDEX

Illustrations are in *italics*.

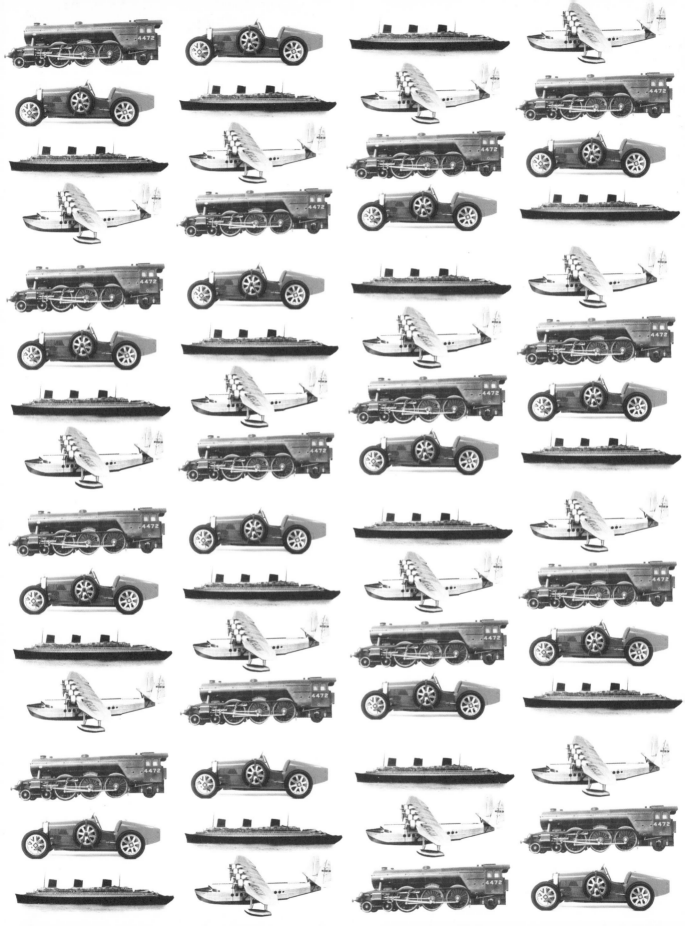